D0399439

THE
AI-FIRST
COMPANY

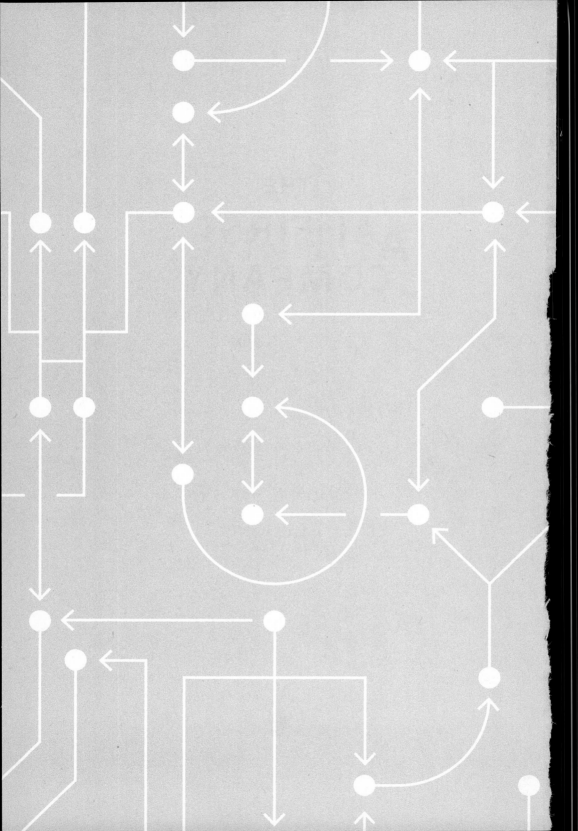

THE
AI-FIRST
COMPANY

HOW TO COMPETE
AND WIN WITH
ARTIFICIAL
INTELLIGENCE

ASH FONTANA

PORTFOLIO | PENGUIN

Portfolio / Penguin
An imprint of Penguin Random House LLC
penguinrandomhouse.com

Most Portfolio books are available at a discount when purchased in quantity for sales
promotions or corporate use. Special editions, which include personalized covers,
excerpts, and corporate imprints, can be created when purchased in large quantities. For
more information, please call (212) 572-2232 or email specialmarkets@
penguinrandomhouse.com. Your local bookstore can also assist with discounted bulk
purchases using the Penguin Random House corporate Business-to-Business program.
For assistance in locating a participating retailer, email B2B@penguinrandomhouse.com.

Grateful acknowledgment is made for permission to reprint the following:
Design and visualization for artwork on pages 24, 54, 77, 93, 94, 95, 140, 174, 195, 196, 205, 206,
208, and 234 by June 10th Creative Services.
All other artwork copyright © 2020 by Fabiola Reina Design. All rights reserved.

Library of Congress Cataloging-in-Publication Data
Names: Fontana, Ash, author.
Title: The AI-first company : how to compete and win with artificial
intelligence / Ash Fontana.
Description: [New York, New York] : Portfolio/Penguin, [2021] |
Includes bibliographical references and index. |
Identifiers: LCCN 2020053301 (print) | LCCN 2020053302 (ebook) |
ISBN 9780593330319 (hardcover) | ISBN 9780593330326 (ebook)
Subjects: LCSH: Business—Data processing—Management. | Artificial
intelligence—Industrial applications.
Classification: LCC HF5548.2 .F57 2021 (print) | LCC HF5548.2 (ebook) |
DDC 658/.0563—dc23
LC record available at https://lccn.loc.gov/2020053301
LC ebook record available at https://lccn.loc.gov/2020053302

Printed in the United States of America
1   3   5   7   9   10   8   6   4   2

To the curious ones

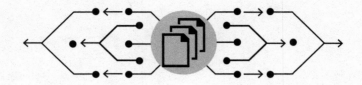

CONTENTS

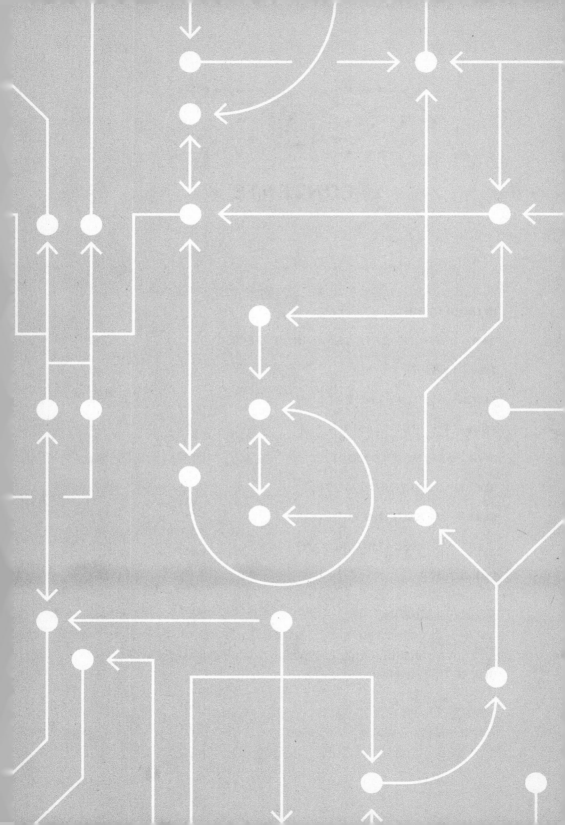

INTRODUCTION

The animal kingdom is full of creatures with better senses than us humans. We can't see like owls or smell like dogs or hear like whales, nor can we do arithmetic faster than a computer—a creature of our own creation. But we are great at gathering a lot of *information* across our senses and processing it in parallel to learn fast. This—learning fast—is the definition of intelligence.

Now artificial intelligence (AI) can help us learn faster by gathering valuable *data*, processing it into information, and spreading it across networks. Companies that build AI increase their own intelligence. That's what this book is all about: building AI-First companies with extraordinary capabilities of gathering, processing, and communicating information to where it's needed, when it's needed—to learn faster than the competition.

AI-First companies were the first—and are still the only—trillion-dollar companies, and they will dominate more industries more definitively than ever before.

This is your guide to building an AI-First company.

THE NEW TOOLS

We like to make new tools and, by doing so, power through our natural limits. Charles Babbage, who arguably invented the first mechanical computer, said, "It is not a bad description of man to describe him as a tool-making animal." We use our intelligence to learn how things work and build tools to make them work better—turning the gradual evolution of man into the fast revolution of man plus machine.

The first wave of tools, during the Stone Age, at least 2.6 million years ago, brought physical leverage. Think rope traps and spears. These allowed us to go beyond our immediate, physical reach to gather more food than we could with our bare hands. The industrial era of the eighteenth and nineteenth centuries brought us increasingly complicated sets of tools that worked in harmony to plow fields and mill steel. However, this physical leverage and scale were limited by our intellectual capacity.

The second wave brought intellectual leverage. The printing press distributed information, but then computers allowed us to gather more information and perform computations beyond our ordinary intellectual reach. We learned how to move information around, throw it into a calculator, quickly send it to different places, and generate multiple insights. However, this intellectual leverage was limited by how much information we could acquire about the future.

Artificial intelligence brings the third wave of tools that give us decision-making leverage. These tools are affording us an entirely new form of intelligence that gathers, processes, and communicates information to make better decisions. We're learning better and faster as we see these decisions play out.

Let's thread a needle: in the first wave, it was possible to stitch fabrics faster than we could weave by hand using looms full of little levers. Physical leverage. In the second wave, computers turned drawings—visual information—into patterns for the loom to automatically weave. Informational leverage. The third wave changes the game: computers scan photos posted on social media, figure out consumer trends, draw up new styles and turn drawings into patterns for the loom. New styles hit the stores right as they become fashionable. Temporal leverage.

Whereas earlier tools gave us physical and intellectual leverage, AI provides decision-making leverage that fulfills two important imperatives. The first applies to all of society: getting more out of our limited resources. The second applies to businesses: building a competitive advantage. Whereas land, labor, and capital were the resources leveraged to compete in the last millennium, information is now the resource to leverage. Whereas the leading companies of yesterday excelled at managing land, labor, and capital, tomorrow's leaders will excel at managing information.

There are many books about using land, labor, and capital to win at business. This book is about using information to win.

THE AI-FIRST CENTURY

The AI-First Century started in 1950 with the development of AI and will finish around 2050 with AI being fully deployed across all industries, so it's not too late for you to get started on applying AI in your industry.

The First Half of the AI-First Century: 1950–2000

If the first fifty years, from 1950 to 2000, were about getting AI to work in the lab, then the next fifty are about getting AI to work for people, business, and society. Understanding how it took the better part of a century to get to this point makes recent innovations seem even more remarkable and highlights our readiness to integrate AI with business strategy. We've thought AI was just around the corner for a long time, but it turns out that it was just getting started, and we are only now bringing working AIs into the real world.

Here is the story of the people who built AI, bit by bit, over the last half century. They are the ones who got us here, and you are the one who will take their work forward over the next half century with the help of this book.

Theoretical Foundations

The foundational thinking about AI happened in the 1950s. Individuals experimented, thought partners collaborated on equations, and groups of great thinkers formed to define artificial intelligence.

Mathematician Warren McCulloch and neurologist Walter Pitts wrote the first equations representing what happens in our minds. McCulloch was educated on the streets of Detroit; Pitts, at an East Coast private school. Both were founding members of the *cybernetics* movement: the science of control and communication in machines and living things. Walter was particularly prodigious, invited to study at England's Cambridge University when he was just twelve after mailing corrections to the great British philosopher and mathematician Bertrand Russell's *Principia Mathematica*, a three-volume work on the foundations of mathematics. He ran away from home when he was fifteen to visit Russell at the University of Chicago and never saw his family again.

Even though Warren was twenty-four years older than Walter, they spent a lot of time together across societies formed to understand the human mind and through institutions such as Massachusetts Institute of Technology (MIT). They also drank a lot of whiskey together. Their partnership yielded an important model known as the *threshold logic unit (TLU)*: a mathematical model of a human brain cell, or *neuron*, that explains how the brain computes things. This model of the atomic unit of our own intelligence provided the starting point for creating artificial intelligence.

Neuroscientists, computer programmers, and researchers from a wide range of disciplines formed groups to discuss how our brain works, and how to represent its functionality—first on paper and then in a computer program. These discussions borrowed concepts from logic, computation, neuroscience, communication, and much more. One group at Dartmouth College coined the term *artificial intelligence* in 1956; another at Cornell University created a *perceptron* algorithm that improved the ability of the earlier algorithms to mimic human neurons; and one at Stanford University joined these neurons together in an early, small version of an *artificial neural network.*

The fifties also brought us the first consideration of how to use AI outside the lab, with the great Alan Turing coming up with a test for intelligence based on reaching a human-level quality of conversation. All the while, Pitts was studying frogs. Among his discoveries: the fact that different parts of a nervous system each carries out a degree of computation. The decade was foundational for AI theory, but the practice was just getting started.

Progressing to Practice

In the 1960s, research on thinking progressed to sensing and speaking. Researchers at MIT, the US Defense Department's Defense Advanced Research Projects Agency (DARPA), and International Business Machines (IBM) studied how neurons move when sensing and reacting to stimuli in the environment, and they wrote computer programs to understand natural language, vision, and reasoning. Around this time, computers learned to play chess—an enduring fascination for the rest of the century.

Government funding for the field was cut in the seventies because developing a general purpose AI was deemed to be an intractable problem, prone to combinatorial explosion. This was more of a political than technological problem: the field overpromised and under-delivered. Corporations picked up the slack, developing the first robots, speech recognition systems, and language translators. Corporations anticipated AI intersecting with another trend: *process automation*. This trend was based on a factory management system developed in the late nineteenth century by an engineer named Frederick W. Taylor. The system increased efficiency by breaking down each step of a manufacturing process into specialized tasks, repeatedly performed by the same person. The trend continued into the twentieth century as specialized tasks could be written in computer code, and then repeatedly performed by computers. At this time, companies such as IBM and Systems Applications and Products in Data Processing (SAP), the German software corporation founded by a former IBM employee in 1972, started making lots of money selling computers to large manufacturing companies that would, for example, log inventory as it moved through a production process. The US military took this a step further to improve logistics: for example, using AI to allocate critical supplies across bases during the 1991 Gulf War against Iraq. Intelligent systems formed, bit by bit, as both companies and governments used AI to automate manufacturing processes and optimize supply chains.

Investment led to innovations in cars (1995), chess (1997), and cute dogs (1999). These breakthroughs were remarkable because they brought AI into the public consciousness, applying it, respectively, to a robot that changed its behavior based on what it could see; the first car to drive itself a thousand miles; the first chess program to beat a world champion; and a "pet" robot that responded to human expressions.

This period resembles what's happening today, twenty years

later: evidence that AI works in the real world—both for the sake of entertainment and to make businesses more efficient—catalyzes investment. However, the investment in AI following the remarkable developments in the nineties didn't lead to many companies adopting AI. The military, IBM, and Sony were among the only entities with enough data, talent, and computing power to build AI at this stage.

These companies had a tremendous head start but were limited by the computing power and networking technology then available. Decades of research led to programmable artificial neurons. However, these programmable artificial neurons were singular and therefore had limited functionality: data in, compute something, data out. Stringing neurons together into large networks required prohibitive amounts of computational resources, which made the approach rather impractical. Architecting and running such a system remained a daunting challenge.

AI researchers made breakthroughs in stringing neurons together in a network at the start of the millennium. The Canadian computer scientist Yoshua Bengio devised a language model based on a neural network that figured out the next best word to use among all the available words in a language based on where that word usually appeared with respect to other words. Geoffrey Hinton, a British-born computer scientist and psychologist, developed a neural network that linked many *layers* of neurons together, the precursor to *deep learning*. Importantly, researchers worked to get these neural networks running efficiently on the available computer chips, settling on the chips used for computer graphics because they are particularly good at running many numerical computations in parallel. The result was a trainable neural network: programmable neurons, connected in a weblike network, passing the computations onto another web sitting below it—all computed on a chip that could perform the necessary operations on a reasonable timescale: mere days instead of months.

Computers Get Cheap

As tends to happen in the world of technology, an innovation in one field sparked innovation in another. The computer science of distributed systems enabled us to build very big, powerful, and cheap computers. This development was the first key enabler of AI. Large technology companies such as IBM and Microsoft gave their customers access to cloud computing clusters, and computing power became cheap as those clusters scaled up. The vast majority of people in the developed world got a computer to carry around. The data created while using these computers and the Internet was the second key enabler of AI. Researchers, equipped with more computing power and data, took a renewed interest in AI. These neural networks became deployable enough to embed in everyday products, from the keyboard on mobile phones, to shopping websites, to devices that sit in our homes such as the Amazon Alexa or Apple HomePod, ready for our every command.

I started working with AI-based technology around the time that researchers began taking an interest in it again, just after the establishment of cloud computing, when lots of data came into the world. Realizing just how much new data was flooding into the world and the challenges of making sense of it all, I started a company that helped the biggest travel companies in the world organize all the data that consumers generated with their phones and on social media. I was in awe of both the progress made and the novelty of deep neural networks. This was a technology that would change *everything* and was well worth spending decades understanding. Indeed, I joined the first investment fund completely focused on AI, Zetta Venture Partners, which was launched in 2013—the same year a whole *zettabyte* of data (10^{21} bytes, or 1 trillion gigabytes) went across the Internet for the first time. We've reviewed tens of thousands of pitches to create AI-First companies, backed pioneering companies, and were the largest investor in the biggest community of *machine learning (ML) engineers* in the world: Kaggle. My job, as a venture capital investor, is to predict as best I can when the frontier of technology meets reality. I've bet my career that, for AI, that time is now. Zetta has since backed the first generation of companies applying AI to the real world, learning lessons as the "rubber hit the road." This book shares those lessons with you.

The Second Half of the AI-First Century: 2000–2050

The last few centuries have shown that a field moves forward when it intersects with another: philosophy and mathematics intersected to generate physics; when industrial engineering and electrical engineering intersected, factories leaped forward in terms of efficiency. Today artificial intelligence is intersecting with *distributed systems*, allowing us to run *machine learning (ML) models* over lots of data, on powerful computers. This book will provide best practices around investing in infrastructure and people that properly understand both intersecting technologies.

It's not too late to build an AI-First company. The rising tide of technology can help you catch up fast, whether you're steering a small boat or a large boat. Contemporary methods efficiently prepare data, let you do a lot with small amounts of data, synthetically generate data, efficiently label data, automatically build ML models, and integrate them with existing software. We will learn about many of these methods in this book.

THE AI-FIRST COMPANY

AI-First companies put AI to work, prioritizing it within real budgets and time constraints. AI-First companies make short-term trade-offs to build intelligence in order to gain a long-term advantage over their competitors.

Over these pages, you will learn answers to the most fundamental questions about running an AI-First company. From the starting points of experimentation and team building to the tactics of implementation, measuring value, and weighing long-term strategic advantage, you will learn what it takes to capture data, mold it for models, and learn faster than the competition.

This book fills the gap between theoretical writing about the potential of AI and technical writing about how to implement AI, offering readers an executable guide to applying AI to business problems. It is designed to be helpful for readers with different degrees of expertise. It offers a primer on AI, a glossary of key terms, and explanations of the component technologies to provide common understanding. The point is not to make you a technical expert but to give you a foundation for better business decision-making. Simply put, this book is about how to use AI to win at business. The question isn't whether you *can* contribute in the AI-First Century but whether you want to.

THE EIGHT-PART FRAMEWORK

The framework is organized into eight chapters, each one building upon the one before it.

1. We define *data learning effects (DLEs)*, the new type of competitive advantage that arises as we move from human

to machine intelligence. This new concept builds upon three existing concepts of competitive advantages: network, scale, and *learning effects*.

2. We show you how to get started today using the concept of *Lean AI*, a methodology for building AIs to test with customers.

3. Now that you've tested AI with customers, we flesh out your strategy for getting more of the data that models need.

4. We give you a plan for building an AI-First team that processes data.

5. With more data, you can build better models to compound the value of that data.

6. Moving from experimentation to production involves deeper integration with your customers' systems and constant management of the models. We give you frameworks for successful customer implementations and a systematic approach to managing AI models.

7. With everything in motion, we have to make sure AI delivers results. We give you qualitative and quantitative ways to measure the models, and the success of your AI-First company.

8. We explore how to aggregate data learning effects with other competitive advantages to build a company that beats *incumbents* and is defensible for decades to come.

	CHAPTER	LESSON
Strategy *What creates a competitive advantage?*	1. Defining Data Learning Effects	• Intelligence is determined by how fast you learn, and you'll learn faster using machines. • The automatic compounding of information is a data learning effect. • Data learning effects = economies of scale to data + data processing capabilities + data network effects. • Data learning effects compound faster than any other form of competitive advantage. • *Data network effects* are where each incremental data point adds more information to a user of the network than the last data point.
Tactics *Where do I start?*	2. Lean AI	• Anyone, at any company, can start building AI. • Lean AI is a process to build an AI-First product.
Capital *How do I allocate resources?*	3. Getting the Data 4. AI-First Teams 5. Making the Models	• The most significant source of data for AI-First companies is from the customers they're serving. • Data coalitions create a unique data asset for both vendors and customers. • AI-First companies need a diverse group of people to manage different technologies. • AI-First companies embed AI-First teams everywhere.

	CHAPTER	LESSON
Metrics *What should happen?*	6. Managing the Models 7. Measuring the Loop	• The world is always changing, so your models will too. • Model management is not code management. • The goal of tracking every version of a model is reproducibility. • The motion of a data learning effect is looping. • *Data learning effects* automatically generate assets, capabilities, and information. • Companies need new methods to properly account for the cost of delivering an AI-First product.
More *What's the second act?*	8. Aggregating Advantages	• *Vertical integration* gets more data, revenue, and profit. • Aggregating data creates new products. • Strategic data management can lead to customer lock-in. • Increase compatibility or create an ecosystem of third-party developers to contribute data to the ecosystem around a product. • Intelligent systems can analyze large amounts of product usage data to personalize products at scale. • *Intelligent applications* borrow from and then subordinate *legacy applications*.

Whether you're a new online retailer, own a family business, or manage a Fortune 500 company, you'll find what you need to compete and win with AI in this book.

Now, let's start building!

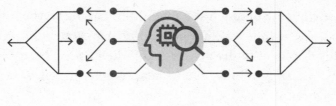

DEFINING DATA LEARNING EFFECTS

O ur fascination with what we have in our head—a mass of neurons, connected together, sitting in fluid, surrounded by membranes and bone, sprouting branches to muscles—led us to develop representations of neurons outside our head, first as logic equations on paper and then as programs that run on computers. The power of AI derives from running these programs on more powerful computers, with more data, across bigger networks, to learn faster. When we change what we use to learn, we can change how fast we learn. We can become more intelligent.

This is all very exciting, and yet we don't have a vocabulary to describe what it means for companies, the economy, and the world. Vocabulary is important because it helps us identify things and figure out knowledge gaps. Analogies can be helpful, but they don't go far enough. People tried to define AI in terms of scale, referring to data as the "new oil"—maybe because oil is an input, and the more of it you have, the better. People also tried to define AI in terms of networks, talking about data network effects—maybe because social networking was a major trend at the start of the big-data era. But neither scale nor network effects capture the power of AI. They don't get to the definition of intelligence: learning fast. Now that we know more about what's possible with AI, we can settle on a vocabulary.

This book provides that vocabulary, starting with a new type of competitive advantage called *data learning effects*: the automatic compounding of information. We learn as we observe. Machines can now observe and learn at a rate and scale far beyond us. Let's briefly consider the human learning formula before laying out the machine learning formula. This chapter defines DLEs, compares them to other types of competitive advantage—the old formulas for competing—and highlights some of their special qualities. Namely, how DLEs lead to winner-take-all dynamics in a market, make products more useful, compound faster than network effects, drive cost leadership, and allow for intelligent product pricing. Finally, we note some of the limitations of DLEs.

THE HUMAN FORMULA

We are very good at gathering data across our senses and processing it in parallel. We learn by processing that input into useful information as soon as it starts moving through our nervous system and thinking it through in relation to what we already know. The new lessons are derived from old lessons. Similarly, machines can learn by gathering data through sensors, processing it into new information, linking it to old information, then doing a lot of mathematics over the old and new information to learn something new. The new lessons are derived from what's in the database. The processes for both humans and machines start with going broad, observing what's out there, then going deep, connecting and relating it to other information to learn something new.

Human learning power comes from collecting information across and between generations. Humans pass on what we learn from one generation to the next, so that we don't have to learn it all over again. One generation invented the hammer, another flattened it into a shovel, and the next molded it into an axe. Humans also pass on information across generations, to each other, every day, peer to peer. The ability to get information from a collective—a network—and derive new information from it is a form of cooperation across time and space. This allows for compounding growth because we're not always going backward to relearn things, slowing our learning. The more you know, the more you *can* know; the more information you can access across your network, the faster you learn.

THE MACHINE FORMULA

Machines can now form collectives—networks—to compute information as well. Previously, machines merely calculated things and maybe stored the output in a database, doing the same calculation when they got new input. Machines can now put that output into a computer, run calculations to turn data into information, and learn over new information. This learning compounds fast with the addition of new information and makes the third wave of tools powerful.

The steps to building a data learning effect with intelligent machines are (1) capturing a critical mass of data, (2) developing capabilities to process that data into information, and (3) feeding that information into a computer that runs calculations over data to learn something new.

Here's the formula:

data learning effects = economies of scale to data + data processing capabilities + data network effects.

Put in a sentence: get lots of data, process it into something useful in terms of making a decision, and create a system that automatically generates more useful data. This is the simple equation and all that's needed to understand the rest of this book; you can skip the four equations below. For those wanting to play around with the concept in more mathematical terms, phrase it in terms of a function that generates output:

> output = function(data, data processing capabilities, data network effects).

Think of this as an order of operations that produces an output:

> output = function(data network effect(processed data quality(data amount))).

Taking a derivative with respect to data allows us to calculate the marginal value of data:

> marginal product of data = value of data network effects x (increase in value of the network per additional unit of data processing x increase in value of processed data per additional unit of data).

Take the log of both sides, and divide by the initial output to get to a formula that tells us how much incremental output comes from incremental data:

> percentage increase in output from more data = log(value of data network effects) + log(value of processed data to a data network) + log(economies of scale to data).

This articulation of the concept shows:

- that this is a *value chain*, with multiple steps to generating increased output;

- the value of each part of the chain depends on the other parts of the chain, e.g., commodity data requires a high degree of processing and augmentation by the network to turn into a valuable asset whereas differentiated data requires less of the same; and

- the sequence of data collection, process, and building network effects.

Data generates marginal output when combined with data processing capabilities and data network effects.

Business strategy vernacular defines DLEs this way:

data learning effects = supply-side input advantage + supply-side process advantage + demand-side increasing returns to scale.

DLEs are possible today because of the recent change in the three substrates.

Economies of scale to data: there is lots of data going across the Internet, captured from the sensors on personal and industrial devices;

Data processing capabilities: very powerful computers that can run calculations over this data, at a reasonable cost, and capable people who can make connections between disparate datasets; and

Data network effects: researchers found ways to organize data into networks that run calculations on one part of the network, send the result to another part of the network for more calculations, and come up with new information. This is the field of neural networks or, more broadly, intelligent systems.

With all three substrates, DLEs can grow. We now work through each of these substrates, contrasting them with contemporary concepts.

BEYOND THE OLD FORMULAS

Data learning network effects are the defining feature of an AI-First company and compound faster than other forms of competitive advantage, but we've struggled to define them until now. We thought machines could learn the same way we do, but machines have a different type of intelligence, so *learning effects* isn't an accurate term. We thought that more data is always better, but not all data can be processed into information. We thought that everything was a network effect after seeing social networks grow fast, and so we thought that AI was a data network effect, too, but that's only one component of the concept and doesn't capture all of its power. DLEs are not the same as learning effects, *scale effects*, or *network effects*. The following sections develop our vocabulary beyond what we have today.

Beyond Learning Effects

Economists study and quantify learning effects, the process through which information accumulation leads to an economic benefit. Think of a management consulting firm that develops strategic frameworks, best practices, and resource allocation models from information accumulated across all of its clients. Traditional learning effects accumulate:

- information on individuals *or* organizations;
- structured *or* unstructured information;
- when information is processed by people *or* machines; and
- a qualitative *or* quantitative benefit.

Traditional learning effects have limits: they grow slowly be-cause unstructured information, such as an image or free-form text, must be processed or structured by a human before it can be processed by a machine. Humans can process only certain types of information, and organizations generally limit the internal and ex-ternal flow of information.

DLEs can accumulate information:

- across single or multiple organizations;

- that is structured;

- when processed by machines; and

- that has a quantitative benefit.

DLEs have very few limits: they grow fast because structured in-formation feeds into machines that calculate faster than humans. Modern computing machines can process multiple types of infor-mation. Learning fast is smart.

Learning effects were for the knowledge economy: the era that started after the industrial revolution, when we moved from man-ufacturing to services. DLEs are for today's economy. This is the era in which we've made several leaps: distributing information digi-tally instead of verbally; sharing information automatically rather than manually; learning across minds instead of learning merely manually; learning on hardware (computers) as opposed to "wet-ware" (brains); and learning not just on one *node* but across nodes in a network. This is the AI-First era.

Beyond Scale Effects

Supply-side returns to scale are a traditional source of competitive advantage. That is, from a supplier's perspective, when the product gets cheaper to supply with the accumulation of assets or capabilities. For example, the large cloud providers offer computing power at a very low relative cost because they can purchase computer chips in bulk, invest in systems to cool the chips to their efficient operating temperature, and negotiate cheaper power with municipalities. This is commonly referred to as a scale effect because increased scale can lead to lower costs, reduced prices, increased demand, thus getting more scale, and so on. This is not a network effect (explained below) because linking the computers together doesn't make them more useful to the customer (although it may make it easier to share networking resources, and thus cheaper to run). Nor is it primarily a learning effect because the cost advantage comes from scale (although there is some accumulated expertise in designing the computing systems and centers).

There are scale effects with data; having a big bucket of data can be a competitive advantage. For example, when selecting a vendor of phone numbers for sales targets, go with the vendor that has the most phone numbers. However, more data only makes a product useful *up to a point*, after which it has less utility because it's effectively the same data. This is why economies of scale to data are just the start of—but not all of—a DLE.

The distinction between data and information informs whether data has marginal utility. Information is measured in how much uncertainty it resolves to the receiver. Information informs whereas data doesn't need to be informationally useful—it's a fact. Not all data contains information; if data cannot be used to change someone's mind—to resolve uncertainty—it's not information. Further, data (facts) are in the real world, but information (distilled, useful, actionable) is in the mind. AI-First companies gather data and use internal capabilities to process it into information using AI minds. Many companies gather loads of data. Only AI-First companies process that data into information that helps answer questions such as "What should I watch next?" "What should this insurance cost me?" "When will I run out of rice?"

One way that data becomes information is by interacting with other bits of data. These interactions often happen across a network, each node interacting with another, having an effect on each other. This is called a network effect. The telephone network is an example of a network effect: when you call someone on the phone, you are interacting with them in such a way as to have an effect on them. For example, let's say I call to tell you that Amelia broke her leg. You in turn call Bruno, a close friend of Amelia's, to ask him to visit Amelia with you. You've had an effect on Bruno. All of you are nodes in a network, and information is shared from person (node) to person, each influencing the other, turning data in one person's head into information in another person's head. The whole group grows and learns as a result.

Data can also be nodes on a network, and when data interacts with other bits of data on the network, it has an *effect* on that data. This interaction usually happens through an interface or protocol that determines the effect. With respect to data networks, data can:

- *integrate* with other data through an *interface* such as an algorithm that combines data;

- *communicate* by sending information (processed data) to other parts of the network over a *protocol* that determines the format; and

- *contribute* to the network when there is an *incentive* to contribute.

For example, neural networks provide an interface for data in the form of an algorithm containing functions that manipulate data. Analyzing these interfaces, protocols, and incentives can help determine if they turn data into information to add to the network. When more data doesn't add information to the network, it is *not* a network effect.

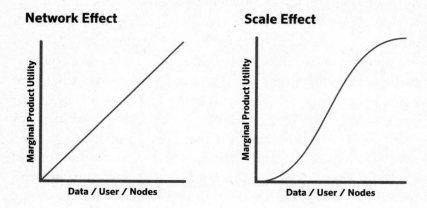

NETWORK VERSUS SCALE EFFECT

Beyond Network Effects

Network effects are said to occur when, from a consumer's perspective, a product becomes more useful as more people use it. Again, the telephone offers a clear example of this kind of network effect. It is useless if you're the only one with a telephone but very useful if many people have one. The effect of more demand is a larger network, leading to more demand for the product, increasing the size of the network, and so on.

DLEs combine three types of competitive advantage: scale, processing capabilities, and network effects. Just having a network effect doesn't mean that a user learns anything. The difference between a network effect and a *data* network effect is what's added to the network. With a network effect, something becomes more useful through the addition of communicative nodes to the network, whereas with a *data* network effect, something's usefulness is enhanced by the addition of data to the network. What's more, a network effect's *edges*—the lines between nodes—are functional and communicate, as opposed to a data network effect's edges, which are informational and calculate. The following diagram shows a network on the left generating data on the nodes (circles) and communicating it along the edges (lines). On the right, the *data* network holds data on the nodes and does calculus along the edges, delivering information to other nodes on the network.

NORMAL VERSUS DATA NETWORK EFFECTS

Normal Network   Data Network

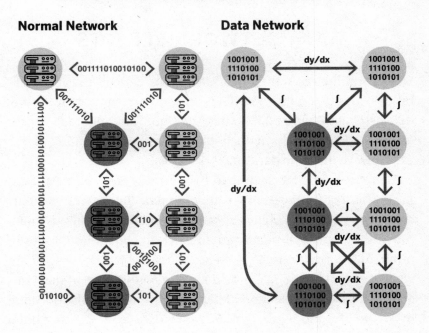

Both are networks: a web of things connected to each other, with information flowing freely through those connections. The network lies underneath a product: sometimes it's simple, like a telephone handset; and other times it's complicated, as with Facebook. Those products themselves are sometimes defensible—the design of a telephone handset can be patented, and the software around a social network is intellectual property (IP)—but the network itself is a *defensible* asset, or protectable source of income. This is the same with a data network—it lies underneath a product: sometimes a simple one, such as a catalogue full of product information; and sometimes a complicated one, like an industrial robot at a

Tesla factory. The distinction between a product with network effects and one without is that the product is more useful because of the network effect. The distinction between a normal network and a data network is that data networks transmit derivatives of data—information—not just data itself.

DATA NETWORK EFFECTS

DLEs combine economies of scale to data, data processing capabilities, and data network effects. We provide tactics for scaling data assets in Chapter 3, "Getting the Data," and methods to process that data throughout the book, starting with Chapter 2, "Lean AI." Now we dive into data network effects.

Data network effects come in two forms: entry and next level. Each requires a different investment in data, talent, and partnerships. *Entry-level data network effects* are when the addition of data provides a marginal benefit to an existing collection of data in terms of information value. *Next-level data network effects* are when the addition of data provides a *compounding* marginal benefit to an existing collection of data in terms of information value by virtue of a model that creates new data from existing data, such as a machine learning model. The first is direct; the second, indirect. Entry-level effects are easier to build: just add information to the network by getting users, customers, and partners to contribute information. Next-level effects, however, require building something else that automatically multiplies the size of the network, such as a system that generates its own information. The reward for leveling up is faster growth, because the network has this second, multiplying factor that compounds the competitive advantage. The following table shows the relative investments in data, technology, talent, customers, and partnerships required.

	ENTRY LEVEL	NEXT LEVEL
Data	High	Low
Technology	Low	High
Talent	Low	High
Customers	High	Low
Partnerships	High	Low

Building an entry-level data network effect would, for example, require gathering a lot of information on customer product preferences. Solid business development representatives can strike deals to get product purchase information. Building a next-level data network effect, on the other hand, may not require manually gathering information but may require building an ML model that learns customer preferences by observing their purchases and then inferring preference information thereafter.

Traditional network effects are entry-level network effects. The value of the network is the number of nodes (n) added over time (t) squared and then multiplied by a constant (C). This assumes that the marginal value of an additional node in the network remains constant, but this is often not true in the real world because networks often have diminishing utility beyond a certain size.

$$Network\ Value_t = C * n_t^2$$

Data network effects are sometimes like this, but sometimes they level up with the addition of automatically generated information to the network. Leveling up changes the exponent in the above equation to a number higher than 2, making the network value grow even faster.

Entry-Level Data Network Effects

Data network effects start when the addition of information to a network makes the product on top of the network more useful. This doesn't involve AI. This information is exogenous to the network: new information, coming from the outside. Think about a simple table of data, then add another row of data to that table; the table is now more useful because it has more data to analyze and turn into information. The decision is made in the mind, but with more data to analyze, it may yield a better decision. These entry-level data network effects are powerful when the information helps to make a better decision.

ENTRY-LEVEL DATA NETWORK EFFECTS

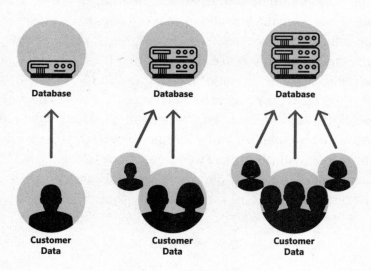

The big-data era, covering roughly the second decade of the twenty-first century, was essentially about these entry-level data network effects. This era saw the development of technology to store, manage, analyze, and visualize very large volumes of data.

These entry-level data network effects happen, in practice,

when products effectively gather and present information to consumers. Here's one simple example: shopping online is better when you have more selection *and* more of an ability to select. The offline version of this is a department store where you have lots of products in one place and store associates to help you select from those products. More selection comes from sourcing inventory—this isn't the data network effect. More of an ability to select comes from gathering, structuring, and presenting information on those products—this is the data network effect. E-commerce sites with information on each product—for example, a speaker's frequency range or the battery life of an electric toothbrush—are good places to shop. Often, the product data takes the form of consumer reviews. Each review is a piece of information that gives you a broader perspective on that product, enhancing your ability to make a wise purchasing decision. By reading the reviews, you're reaping a benefit from everyone who wrote a review before you. When you buy a product and then write your own review, you kick off the data network effect: the last person who wrote a review affects your purchasing decision and then, if you purchase the product and leave a review, now you're both helping to make the sale to the next person. In this way, entry-level data network effects compound with the addition of exogenous information to the network, so they need information contributed from outside sources to grow.

Next-Level Data Network Effects

Data network effects level up when the addition of data plus something else that generates information—such as AI—makes something more useful. In other words, once these networks have data from outside sources, they generate their own information to grow. This is the power of leveling up: the network effect becomes self-sustaining and can grow at a *multiple* (C, in the equation) of an *exponential* (2, in the equation) rate.

NEXT-LEVEL DATA NETWORK EFFECTS

First Customers

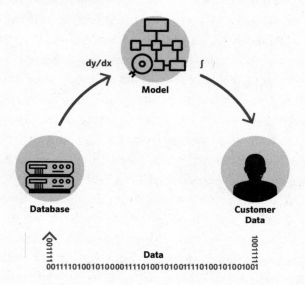

Model

dy/dx ∫

Database

Customer Data

0011111

1001111

Data
001111010010100001110100101001110100101001001

More Customers

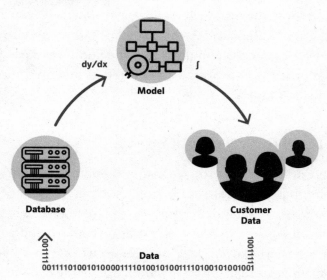

Model

dy/dx ∫

Database

Customer Data

0011111

1001111

Data
001111010010100001110100101001110100101001001

In practice, these happen when each consumer of a product generates data that feeds a system that turns the data into information. The consumers of the product effectively form a network of data contributors, and benefit from the data added by new contributors because it generates information. For example, shopping online often starts with a search, and the shopping experience is better when you find what you want to buy faster. Search engines powered by ML models can use data gathered from what people typed into the search box, clicked on, purchased, and positively reviewed to move products up and down on the search results page—ideally presenting the most relevant result first. The ML models learn as shoppers either click on or ignore the search results.

The Shared Brain

What's really happening with entry-level data network effects is that a person used his or her own neural network (the brain) to accumulate the data, turn it into information, compare it to other information, learn something, make a prediction, make a decision, and then learn more from the effect of that decision. Any leveling up is limited by the neural network in that person's brain. The learning isn't shared; just make a decision and move on.

THE BRAIN WITH INPUTS

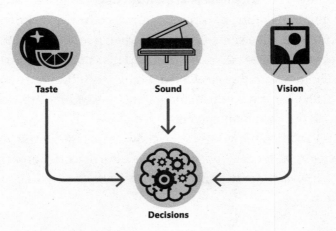

Taste   Sound   Vision

Decisions

For example, you look at a data dashboard showing the types of defects in plastic bottle tops on the production line and compare this with what you saw in the defect bin with your own eyes. You discover that the plastic tops warp every time the temperature exceeds 250°C. From this information, you determine that if you limit the temperature to 250°C, the tops won't warp, and so you decide to implement the limit on the plastic extrusion machine. This might be a good change, but there's no way to learn from it in a systematic or networked way. Maybe you see fewer defects in the future, but maybe you get busy with another project.

The real leveling up occurs when going beyond our own neural network to utilize even bigger collective networks computed at a large scale. The network effect compounds and scales more quickly because it can run on lots of computers, in lots of places, and on more data at the same time.

Using the above example again, you could have a system that changes the temperature by 1°C across multiple production lines at once, measures the defect rate by analyzing images of the plastic lids, then automatically decides on the optimal extrusion temperature. This system uses information from multiple lines, sensors, and computations, then automatically feeds it back into a predictive system that decides on the best experiment to run next.

Entry-level network effects are a form of collective intelligence, in that obtaining more information from a collective of individuals makes for better decisions. This is like when people share information between and across generations. This is our superpower as human beings, and this is what supercharges it into the next century: AI. Sharing more information across the Internet allows us to learn with our own intelligence.

Next-level data network effects allow for a superior form of intelligence that learns faster. Sharing information across these systems allows them to make better decisions *based on* better information.

THE SHARED BRAIN WITH INPUTS

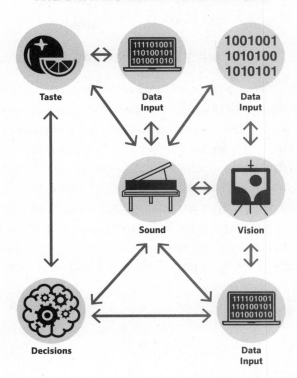

What to Build?

The type of data network effect to build depends on the available data, talent, and customers. There are significant competitive advantages to build at the entry level by adding any data at all. However, this needs more data to increase the value of the network over time—it's not automatic.

Deciding when to level up investment depends on whether the available data can train a self-learning system and if customers will benefit from the predictions that come out of such a system. In either case, both are sufficient to kick off a DLE because the collective intelligence of the system increases with the addition of data to the network.

THE POWERS OF DATA LEARNING EFFECTS

Winners Take All with Data Learning Effects

Markets tip to a single technology when there are both high economies of scale and demand for variety. Economies of scale happen when cost decreases, on a marginal basis, as production increases. Variety is customer demand for lots of different features or products. Referring to the bottom-right quadrant of the table below, customers want variety when shopping online, and operating warehouses gets cheaper as they get bigger, so Amazon dominates e-commerce. Referring to the bottom-left quadrant of the table below, we want variety in our news sources, but journalists can write only so many articles per day—they don't scale well—so there are a few large newspapers.

WINNERS	LOW ECONOMIES OF SCALE	HIGH ECONOMIES OF SCALE
LOW DEMAND FOR VARIETY	Many	Few
HIGH DEMAND FOR VARIETY	Few	One

Only one company accumulates the most resources (like investment, ecosystem participants, among others) in a market, and the company with the most resources is the only one that can invest in building a wide variety of features for that market's customers. The company with the most scale can offer the most variety, so it dominates the market after this tipping point.

DLEs can have high economies of *scale* to data because they need lots of data to get started. DLEs create a wide *variety* of predictions because models are constantly generating different predictions based on feedback data. Further, customers of AI-First products inherently have a high demand for variety because each customer needs a model that can make predictions specific to their business. DLEs thus tip markets in favor of one winner.

Data Learning Effects Make Products More Useful

Data learning effects tend to work behind the scenes rather than front and center. Some products manifest their utility in the foreground and some in the background. Manifesting utility in the foreground means that the increasing utility is obvious to the end user, who sees that adding some data generates a more accurate prediction for them or immediately triggers a new insight. For example, adding their own sales data allows them to immediately see their sales benchmarked against their competitors' sales. Manifesting utility in the background means that increasing utility is not obvious to the user. The user doesn't see that adding some data generates a better prediction for them, and they don't see any information they don't already have.

One product that gets better in the foreground thanks to DLEs is Square Capital, the division of Square that lends money to customers of the company's point-of-sale (POS) systems (their cash registers). Merchants, such as restaurant owners, add data from their POS systems and get loans based on how much money they're making, almost immediately. Square is able to offer them that loan by comparing the data uploaded by the merchant to other merchants that previously received loans from Square. The user (the merchant) sees an immediate benefit of adding data (the offer of a loan) because the product utilizes a DLE to run a predictive system that delivers that product: an interest rate based on the prediction that the merchant will pay back the loan. You don't get a loan if you don't add data, and you qualify for a loan only because your data can be compared with other data to generate a prediction. This product is based on DLEs and gets better in the foreground.

One product that gets better in the background thanks to DLEs is Cloudflare, a website performance and security product. Customers such as news websites add a Cloudflare data collection mechanism to the network, which serves up page requests to the website's viewers and provides protection against requests from bad actors. Cloudflare offers that protection by comparing which requests were bad for other Cloudflare customers, with "bad'" meaning a request that tries to swamp the site with traffic in an attempt to shut it down (a *denial-of-service*, or DoS, attack) or otherwise exploit a security hole. The customer (the website owner) does not see an alert to deny a particularly dangerous request immediately after adding the Cloudflare data collection mechanism, but the product is constantly learning and delivering alerts to potentially bad requests. You don't receive these alerts if you don't allow Cloudflare to see your network requests. The product is based on DLEs and gets better in the background.

Data Learning Effects Compound Faster Than Network Effects

DLEs compound fast when they get data from customers. The fuel for the network effect is data, and customers provide this fuel for the system that ultimately benefits them.

Products with entry-level data network effects often get data customers, sometimes called a *give-to-get* model. Every customer contributes data that may make the product more useful, attracting more customers, and so on. High-quality data makes the product better, and customers can contribute some of that data.

Products with next-level data network effects often get data from customers that provide data as part of using the product, sometimes called *feedback data*, but—crucially—that data goes into a model that compounds the value of this data by transforming it into a prediction.

For example, customers submit data every time they get a credit score, and the credit scoring agencies use the data to provide more accurate scores (and then sell it to third parties). That's an entry-level data network effect. The next level would be a lending application where a customer provides ongoing access to their spending in order to receive loan offers. The company offering the loan can then predict if and when it may be paid back, decide on the customer's creditworthiness, and, accordingly, issue a bigger loan or cut them off. The difference between the two levels is the feedback data and the predictive model.

One Flywheel Kicks Off Another

Automating this process of collecting data and generating information is the start of the next level, when the shared brain starts comparing what it learns to other things it learns. This is the "flywheel" that kicks one network effect into another, more powerful network effect.

Amazon made this happen. First, it gathered a great deal of data on products and helped customers make better buying decisions by putting all of that data in the product listings, providing comparison tables with structured product information. More information meant better comparisons and decisions. Then Amazon invested in a team to build machine learned search and recommendation systems: A9. This team effectively got that product data and matched it with purchase data to learn which products customers want to buy so that Amazon could recommend similar products to those customers in listing pages and search results. Gathering a lot of data started the entry-level network effect: Amazon was the most useful shopping website to consumers because it had the most product information. Learning over that data kicked off the next-level network effect: Amazon is the most useful shopping website to consumers because it offers the best recommendations and has the best search experience.

ONE FLYWHEEL KICKS OFF ANOTHER

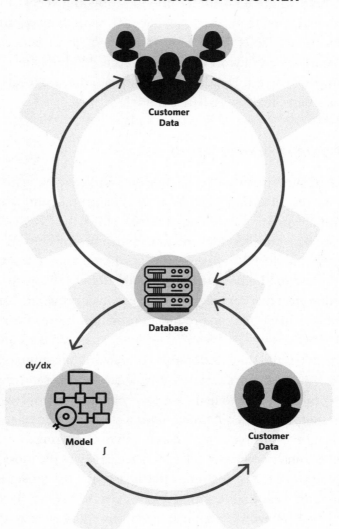

Customer
Data

Database

dy/dx

Model

∫

Customer
Data

Data Learning Effects Drive Cost Leadership

DLEs automatically enable businesses to reduce the cost of making products while also increasing their value for customers. This allows for *cost leadership* by either charging less or charging the same but providing more value.

The initial cost of making products with DLEs amortizes over each additional customer. Building intelligent systems is expensive: buying, collecting, cleaning, and storing data. Hiring data scientists and ML engineers is also expensive. Usually a company has to spend a lot of money before customers see value in the predictions. However, expenses reduce once customers start using the product and contributing data. Customers might label or store their own data, or they might reconfigure the model's features through an interface. Customers effectively take on the cost of gathering and processing data through feedback systems, reducing production and maintenance costs, and allowing for cost leadership.

DLEs make products more valuable. More data empowers customers to make more accurate predictions and better decisions. Improved performance of the underlying models generates value for customers, meaning a higher return on their investments. The denominator (price) stays the same as value goes up.

$$\frac{\text{Revenues from Investment} - \text{Cost of Investment}}{\text{Cost of Investment}} \times 100 = ROI\ (\%)$$

Incidentally, cost leadership may help to quickly build a DLE. Cost leadership is a strategy to attract more customers, who, in turn, generate more data. This strategy may be deliberately employed to the point of unprofitability for a limited period of time to accumulate the critical mass of data required to improve an AI's accuracy so that it is useful to customers.

DATA LEARNING EFFECTS DRIVE COST LEADERSHIP

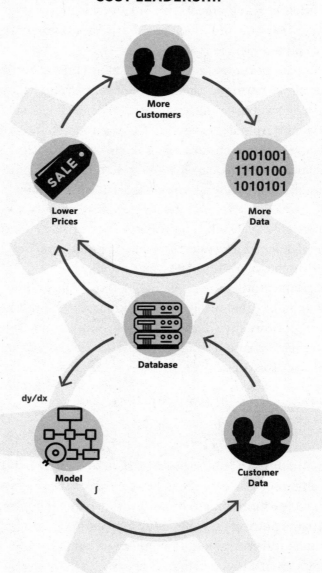

Data Learning Effects and Price Optimization

DLEs allow for more accurate pricing. Well-priced products sell more, and more customers gather more data, powering the DLE. Cost leadership is different from *price optimization*, and better pricing can boost DLEs.

Pricing is an information game that is won by figuring out exactly what someone will pay for something. Predictive systems are used in pricing experiments to generate test prices. One way to run a pricing experiment is to pick a price based on experience, observations, guesses, or other factors. Another way is to use data from previous experiments to predict what is probably an acceptable price. This second approach is more likely to find the optimal price.

E-commerce websites often personalize pricing. The price one shopper sees for a product is often different from the price another sees on the same website, or the price a shopper sees for a product on his phone may be different from the price for the same product when seen on his laptop. This is because the AI constantly runs experiments to see what customers may pay for something based on who they are (if logged in to a profile with previous purchases and demographic information), where they live, what they just clicked on, etc. Sophisticated shopping websites use hundreds of data points on each individual, from sets of data about customer preferences, and billions of data points on different groups of people to price products. These websites often have promotions that might even lose money—selling the product below cost—but which ultimately generate useful data about what customers might be willing to pay.

The *manual personalization process* may involve taking an observation, using it to inform the next price in an experiment, running the next experiment, making more observations, and so on. The *automated personalization process* may entail using ML by feeding data into a system that generates a price to test based on the gradient of the curve it thinks will arrive at the optimal price.

Airlines developed some of the first price optimization systems, commonly known as *yield management systems*, that priced each seat based on variables such as: the number of seats on the plane, the cost of flying that plane on the given route, the seat position, the expected demand given the time of year, and so on. These systems rely on the mathematical concept of linear optimization, the basis of some ML systems. Today these systems price seats, change the prices minute by minute, and distribute those prices to the myriad places to buy plane tickets.

There are also examples of predictive pricing for software products sold to businesses. The challenge is that there's typically less data available on what business customers will pay for a product because they make fewer bigger purchasing decisions and because their behavior when making those decisions isn't as easily observed as consumers browsing a shopping website.

Better pricing leads to more profit and boosting DLEs *if* profits are invested back into DLEs.

- Better pricing yields profit to invest in ML *research and development (R & D)*.

- Better pricing attracts customers, thus more data (at no cost), increasing profit, allowing further investment in R & D.

- Better pricing means less spending on sales and marketing, increasing profit, allowing further investment in R & D.

LIMITATIONS OF DATA LEARNING EFFECTS

There are limits to network effects, calling into question the assumption that utility constantly increases with the size of the network. Sometimes the limitation is external; for example, with regulatory action against the network owner as the product overlaying the network reaches a monopolistic position in the market. Other times the limitation is internal; say, the technology that serves the product around the network breaks at a certain scale. And sometimes the product generating the network effect just doesn't become more useful beyond a certain network size; for instance, your 510th friend on Facebook isn't as nice to have as your 50th friend on Facebook; you just don't engage with them, or the product, as much once the network grows beyond a certain size.

DLEs face limits, too. Sometimes the limits are external, as in the case of regulatory action against the owner of the data by the government to break up the owner's monopolistic position in the market. Sometimes it is internal; for example, if the data becomes too expensive to store and manage. This can even create a situation of decreasing returns to scale of data if adding a data point increases extraction, transformation, preparation, cleaning, loading, and storage costs. For example, adding more data to a customer relationship management system about each customer's preferences creates the need for more fine-grained labels to meaningfully classify the data. Adding data can also increase the required number of output dimensions, in other words, what the prediction must display. Sometimes the product generating the network effect doesn't have marginal utility with the addition of more information; for instance the three hundredth review of a coffee shop on Google Maps or Yelp isn't as useful as the third review; the aggregate score is more solid, but no one reads that three hundredth review. More data isn't always better.

DLEs have limits by virtue of acquiring new data, increasing the cost of building the product, or failing to generate new information. The value of getting more data is a technical and practical consideration: the extra data must make the model more accurate, and that increased accuracy must be useful to customers.

CONCLUSION:
NOW WHAT?

We have vocabulary to describe how companies collectively and quickly learn from data. These companies make the leap from verbally to digitally distributing information, from manually to automatically sharing information, from learning in our own minds to learning across minds, from learning on wetware to learning on hardware, and from learning on one node to learning across nodes in a network. These are AI-First companies.

I've found that network effects just don't happen in AI-First companies the way they do in social networks: starting because one user ropes in others and escalating from there. Data network effects start only after working hard to gather and process data. That sometimes takes years and doesn't happen just by making the right technology choices. Highly capable people who know what data is where and why it's relevant to solving particular problems are crucial. What I've seen companies learn as a result of this hard work is powerful. When the DLE kicks in, not only do they attract more customers, but also they procure *proprietary information* about businesses that can be used to figure out how to automate core processes. This automation makes their customers' businesses more profitable, and this is what makes AI-First products stick.

The following path maps out the learning journey of the AI-First company. First, we learn about how to obtain and value data, then how to build an AI-First team to process that data, and then how to build the models that use that data to improve the product. This gets us a compounding source of competitive advantage in DLEs that can lead to a significant degree of automation. The question then becomes what to do with the cost savings that come from automation, which we cover in the final chapter of the book, "Aggregating Advantages."

THE DATA LEARNING EFFECTS JOURNEY

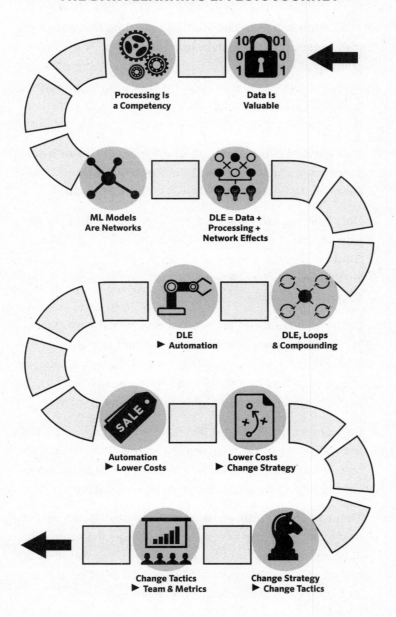

Processing Is
a Competency

Data Is
Valuable

ML Models
Are Networks

DLE = Data +
Processing +
Network Effects

DLE
▶ Automation

DLE, Loops
& Compounding

Automation
▶ Lower Costs

Lower Costs
▶ Change Strategy

Change Tactics
▶ Team & Metrics

Change Strategy
▶ Change Tactics

PLAYBOOK

- **The accumulation of information from data that automatically compounds is a data learning effect.** The steps to building a DLE are: (1) capturing a critical mass of data; (2) developing capabilities to process that data into information; and (3) feeding that information into a computer that runs calculations over data, learning from new data points.

- **Data generates marginal output when combined with data processing capabilities and data network effects.** Data learning effects articulate the value chain around data.

- **Data learning effects are unique.** They start with a supply-side competitive advantage that kicks off a demand-side competitive advantage and combines privileged access to a resource with capabilities to transform that resource into something valuable.

- **Data network effects are not like normal network effects.** The difference between a network effect and a data network effect is what's added to the network. With a network effect, edges are functional and communicate. With a data network effect, edges are informational and calculate.

- **Data scale effects are not just economies of scale to data.** More data doesn't automatically lead to a data network effect, but it may lead to a scale effect, whereby costs of processing or acquiring data decrease as scale increases.

- **There are two types of data network effects: entry and next level.** The entry level sees the addition of data producing a positive effect, but the next level is when the addition of data plus AI causes the positive effect. The first are easier to build, but the second grow faster.

- **Next-level data network effects generate data for free.** Entry-level effects need data from outside the network. Next-level effects generate data from inside the network (feedback data) leading to a high rate of compounding the value of data assets.

- **Better intelligence forms from self-generating data networks.** Entry-level data network effects augment our own intelligence. Next-level data network effects enable faster learning.

- **Winners take all with data learning effects.** AI-First products have high economies of scale to data and high demand for variety between customers such that these products can dominate an industry after a tipping point.

- **Data learning effects make products cheaper.** DLEs allow for cost leadership by reducing the cost of acquiring and processing data while delivering more value to customers.

- **Data learning effects make products easier to price.** Build a separate, intelligent system to run price experiments and optimize pricing across customer segments.

- **Data learning effects have limitations.** DLEs are limited by scaling limits of surrounding technology, data storage costs, lack of marginal utility to customers, and regulatory action.

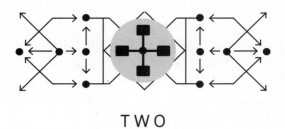

TWO

LEAN AI

L et's take a shortcut to building AI, narrowing the scope of what to do now, ahead of building each component of a DLE. This chapter examines how to get started with the resources you have available while the chapters that follow break down each component of a DLE: getting the data, building the team that processes the data, and building models that generate a data network effect.

Your customers may not need AI at the beginning; some statistical analysis could do the trick. Finally, we provide a new vocabulary to describe the Lean AI method and show how it's different from the vocabulary used to talk about the previous generation of software and startups. Accuracy is performance for AI-First products, and predictions are the product.

The chapters that follow this one put flesh on the bones of a Lean-AI system by covering how to acquire data, build the AI models, create a self-reinforcing loop, and account for the resulting profit from AI.

Remember: anyone, at any company, can start building an AI system. Are you ready?

WHAT DO CUSTOMERS NEED?

Customers won't necessarily say what they need, as per this famous line attributed to automaker Henry Ford: "If I had asked people what they wanted, they would have said faster horses." Product design comes before thinking about AI. This section outlines the principles for designing a product that meets customer needs.

	DEDUCTION	INDUCTION
Research	Calling customers	Running surveys
Design	Design from a specification	Design from intuition
Test	Get feedback from a customer	Run quantitative tests across customer segments
Market	Business	Consumer
Motion	Centripetal	Centrifugal

Figuring out customer demand can be inductive: ask questions, listen, infer what's needed, then build it. Entrepreneurs without much experience in an industry often inductively figure out where the demand lies by asking lots of questions before starting up. The inductive process is focused loosely on getting information from a group of potential customers to both induce a demand trend and come up with a list of features to meet that demand. This typically involves running surveys, coming up with a design to test with different groups of potential customers, and iterating on the design. This is a *centrifugal* process: spinning around lots of data about what people are buying (supply) before settling on what customers need (demand). Many consumer products are designed this way because the potential customer pool is so large.

Figuring out what to supply customers with can be deductive. Entrepreneurs with an existing business often deductively figure out what to supply by seeing what worked in the past and adding new products. The deductive process is focused tightly on getting information from one customer to deduce a supply trend and formulate a list of product features. This typically involves calling customers, coming up with a design, having lots of meetings to refine it, and collecting feedback on the product postimplementation. This is a *centripetal* process: gradually narrow in on a product specification that matches customers' needs. Many business products are designed this way because the number of potential customers is small, so it's possible to talk to all of them.

The next question is: Does the prototypical product need AI to work well? The answer centers on whether customers need to generate an insight, make a prediction, or automate a process.

DO CUSTOMERS NEED AI?

The promise of AI is that it helps to make better, faster decisions. How much AI customers need depends on the types of decisions they're making and the data on which they're basing those decisions. Here is a way to classify the decisions and data on hand that will help to determine if customers need AI or analytics. What type of AI or analytics they need is another matter; this is just the first step, to put the types of decisions and data into two buckets.

THE LEAN-AI DECISION TREE

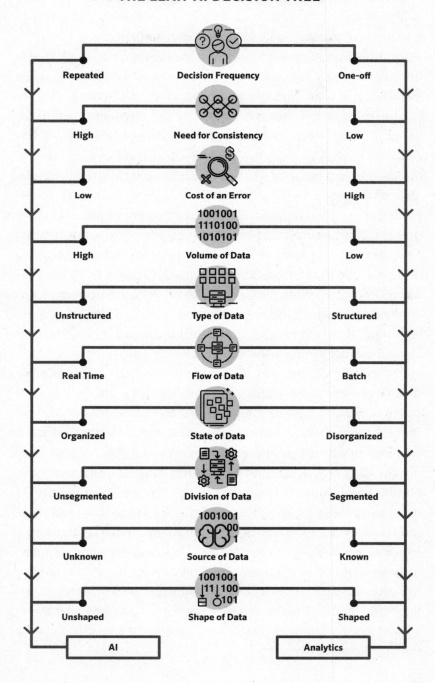

Go through this decision tree and weigh the two buckets: AI and analytics. If analytics is heavier, then it's likely that customers need features on data such as logging, cleaning, and operating—in other words, mathematical operations like averaging—but no AI. If AI is heavier, then it's likely that customers need AI features such as classification, segmentation, and manipulation of data.

The reality is that customers probably need both non-AI and AI-based methods, even if what they eventually need requires AI, because building AI is a gradual, stepwise process. Put another way, the steps before building AI are data engineering and data science. Data engineering includes instrumenting data sources to consistently collect good data, building infrastructure in which to store that data, extracting data from existing data stores, transforming data that doesn't match the structure of existing data, and making it easy to load data into different databases. Data science encompasses detecting anomalies, setting up analytical processes to run on the data at regular intervals, segmenting data, aggregating datasets to put data into context, and figuring out which features of an algorithm might predict something useful.

Then we finally get to AI. This is where we start testing whether those features are predictive of something, run more experiments on more data, design new algorithms, train models, and deploy them in the real world. This will be a joint process with customers: figuring out what they need, whether that's analytics or AI, and doing the data engineering, data science, and ML engineering to build a small model. These tests guide how to package the AI model and build the right team to bring that model to market. AI models are difficult to mock up, unlike, say, software interfaces. One way to do this is to simulate an AI model with a human manually generating, or even guessing, predictions to get a response from customers. Manual work is the natural first step. Seeing, hearing, and feeling what customers want allow us to be smart about where to invest next, and that's likely to be in turning this art into a science: data science.

Starting Small: Statistics

Starting with statistics makes sense when establishing what customers and their data are saying. Customers have questions, data has answers, and data science is the link between the two. Customers say what they want to know, the data shows what they already know, and data science helps extrapolate what they will want to know next from the data.

AI can be a distraction. Throwing a large amount of data into a neural network is unlikely to yield a beneficial result for customers because working with AIs is just hard: needing more data, cleaning data, tuning models, and doing lots of things that don't have anything to do with getting a result for customers on a timeline and budget that works for them.

Instead, there are many non-AI tools to help calculate patterns and determine which components impact others. The first one to pick up could be the data science version of a pencil: plotting structured data on a *histogram* or scatter chart to get a feel for what's happening behind the data. *Clustering*, using *unsupervised ML* to group similar objects, and *dimensionality reduction*, transforming data (using a method such as principal component analysis) to reduce the measures associated with each data point, are the next tools to pick up to pinpoint potential causes—predictive features of an ML model. After figuring out one cause, start playing with combinations of causes by training a *random forest* or a *gradient boosted tree*, then draw *variable importance plots* and *partial plots* to see if the relationships the model is finding make sense. Images, speech, and text may require different approaches that involve picking up pretrained neural networks. Essentially: start by getting one answer with one statistical method. Then use that to arrive at the next answer with another statistical method. AIs eventually emerge.

WHAT WORKS VERSUS WHAT PEOPLE THINK

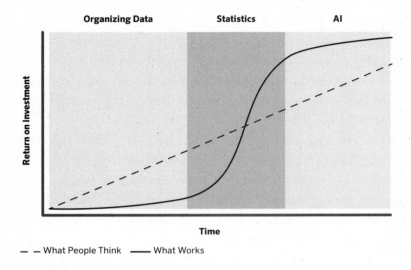

Think about it this way: try one statistical method before layering and intertwining many methods. The latter is a neural network: a web of lots of equations, the results of which feed into other equations on the layer above them, feeding into even more layers above them, and so on. That's the "network" part of a neural network: the interfacing of equations across different layers of abstraction. Before creating a bunch of chatter between equations, have a single conversation with *one equation* to see if it answers customers' questions.

We're not here to build a data science consulting firm, but DLEs start with data science. Most AI models are based on statistical methods. Starting with statistics allows for a smooth transition into AI when there's enough time and money from customers to build it.

Starting Small: Data Science

Starting with a data scientist solving a well-defined problem saves time and money when compared to starting with a team big enough to solve an amorphous problem with machine learning. Dedicate a data scientist to serve as a consultant to customers and provide personalized, data-driven answers to a single question in order to demonstrate *return on investment (ROI)*. Let's contrast this approach with answering multiple questions at once using ML.

	ONE-OFF	SELF-LEARNING
Data acquisition	Manually fetch	Automatically fetch through a direct database connection
Data preparation	None—pick a clean dataset	Clean and label multiple datasets
Storage	Local	Cloud
Data pipeline	One pipeline	Many pipelines
Feature development	Find one feature	Try many features
Training	One calculation	Many calculations
Computation	Local central processing unit (CPU) or graphics processing unit (GPU)	Cloud GPUs
Modeling	One model	Network of models
Deployment	Local	Cloud
Presentation	Print a report	Build an interface

Answering one question means working with one dataset that is likely to have the answer to that question, not gathering data from multiple sources and then cleaning (and labeling) that data. It also entails coming up with one predictive feature to figure out the answer, not multiple features that let an ML model perform the task. Models with one feature can run on a laptop, whereas models with multiple features need more powerful computers. Presenting answers in a printed report requires less engineering than building an interface to change parameters and view answers. Linking databases, cleaning data, creating data pipelines, building features, and designing interfaces is a lot of work, but avoidable work.

There's also evidence that starting with data science works on Kaggle, where the largest community of data scientists and ML engineers compete to win prizes for solving problems. The summary is that data science methods get to the *Pareto optimal solution* (achieving 80 percent of the optimal solution for 20 percent of the work). Often, only the last 20 percent requires data science. Specifically, data science methods such as ensembles of decision trees— whether random forest or gradient boosted—combined with manual feature engineering win most of the competitions on structured data, and neural networks win most of the competitions on unstructured data.

Starting Small: Data

The experimental phase is not the time to build a "fat" data pipeline but rather the time to stay lean, so it's worth making a quick diversion here to talk about getting *just enough* data to build an AI.

Hopefully, this means just one set of data that's located in one database and can be retrieved with a single query. The customer's first guess at which data might be predictive is probably the best starting point because the customer knows their domain better than anyone and may have tried to solve the problem at hand in other ways.

Data preparation comes next and, with any luck, it will be minimal at this stage, taken from one data source. The next step is formatting, with the same units of measurement and file types. Cleaning the data to fill in missing values, delete duplicates, and remove errant values is generally necessary but, again, minimized by obtaining data from a single source. The final step is making sure the data is efficiently computable by the models. Most of the time, this isn't a major consideration with small-scale experiments. Here's what *not* to do, at this stage.

- **DO NOT LABEL EXTENSIVELY.** Determining at the outset what data customers have that might be predictive can spare the time-consuming and costly task of *data labeling*.

- **DO NOT HARVEST DATA FROM MULTIPLE SOURCES.** Doing so requires obtaining extra permissions, building more integrations, and more formatting. Instead, pick one dataset in one data store, run an experiment, then get another only if the dataset doesn't have any predictive power.

- **DO NOT WORK WITH SENSITIVE DATA.** Anonymizing data is costly and may obfuscate results. However, it may be necessary to avoid being held responsible for a data breach.

- **DO NOT BUILD A SEPARATE DATA STORE.** Instead, just download it somewhere secure with low latency, such as a local machine.

- **DO NOT BUILD A DATA PLATFORM.** Decide on all the tools that the entire team will use to explore and manage data. Needs are very likely to change, so consider delaying this choice beyond the initial phase of a project.

The latter point can also be framed around building a "data lake," a term commonly used to describe high volume data storage systems. This serves as a warning about overinvesting in data infrastructure. Yes, most customers have a data-quality problem, with their data located in a multitude of warehouses, incorrectly labeled and missing values. However, now is not the time to solve that problem. Rather, it's time to prove value as a company that can build real working AIs. Later on, when it's necessary for AIs to use data from all over the organization, construct a data lake, adopt a metadata management process, test *ETL (extract, transform, and load)* products that automate some of the data processing steps, manually (re-)label data, hire *data stewards* to ensure compliance with data labeling standards, or implement any number of best practices advocated by large consulting firms and data product vendors. The first job is to provide a useful prediction.

Starting Small: Sales

Beginning with a small, well-defined project makes it easier to build trust with customers, gain access to their data, and learn how they interact with legacy data tools.

Starting small increases buyer engagement because it means working with one stakeholder at a time to answer her most pressing question. Listening to customers' questions and supplying answers promotes trust. Engagement increases when expectations around the power of the model—usually measured by its accuracy—are met, and meeting expectations is easier when solving small, tractable problems. Engagement is stifled, however, when data privacy and security issues come up, but starting with a single dataset can prevent such issues.

Starting small, with a single *question* about data in one dataset, reduces the need to wrestle with poor data from multiple databases. Starting with one *algorithm* reduces the chance that any one part of the solution breaks, because there's only one part to it. Starting with one algorithm also makes deployment relatively simple because there is only one algorithm to sit on top of legacy systems as a view on a dashboard, a calculation at the end of a process, or a rule tacked on to the end of a set of rules already in production.

Starting small means delivering predictions to teams in a way that's easy for them to consume. This is especially important for those who haven't been around AI before. They often want to understand the "why" behind a prediction, and starting small makes explaining the "why" easier. Ask customers how they want to get the answers in order to customize consumption, whether that's through a report, email, spreadsheet, or dashboard.

Sales, models, and products succeed when starting small by answering one question, for one set of stakeholders, using one method. Expand the engagement from there by picking the next best problem to tackle for the most motivated customer.

POV on POC

The question of whether and how to go through a *proof of concept (POC)* phase often comes up with customers because working with consultants, start-ups, or established software vendors takes resources that could be better allocated to a customer's existing businesses. This is why large companies prefer to start with a contained project to prove value.

AI-First products tend to require a POC because the value proposition centers on making an accurate prediction, and potential customers need to know the accuracy of the model when it's running on their data, in their environment. This is different from a standard software product where the value proposition is based on a set of features that are easy to demonstrate and doesn't differ much between vendors.

Running a successful POC requires setting clear expectations around accuracy, timeline, and cost. Briefly, here are the elements of a good POC.

1. **Accuracy:** Set a benchmark for predictions based on honest assessments of what's feasible technically. For example, fully autonomous vehicles are not feasible at the time of this writing, but sensors that detect potholes and alert maintenance crews work quite well. The extrinsic way to set a

benchmark is based on what accuracy a customer already achieved through their own efforts.

2. **Business goal:** This is the metric that gets closest to what customers need to hit to make money. A business generally has a good idea of its goals but sometimes needs help to understand the ways that AI can help it achieve them. Then separate the goals between those to hit during the POC and those to hit in subsequent engagements or phases.

3. **Data:** List the data sources needed and decide if they're accessible. Typically, 80 percent of the time dedicated to building AI is spent preparing data and the other 20 percent is spent creating the models.

4. **Dependency:** Document dependencies on legacy systems, to mitigate problems.

5. **Team:** Limit the team members, to strike a balance between getting enough stakeholder engagement and getting the work done.

6. **Timeline:** Assess what to build, how long it will take, and how long it will take to hit the accuracy benchmark. Help customers understand that getting to 80 percent accuracy may take just 20 percent of the time, but netting that remaining 20 percent may consume 80 percent of the time.

7. **Cost:** Clarify the total cost after figuring out the time required, external consultants, labeling data, and engineering time.

After you've completed the proof of concept phase, come up with a plan on how to reach a higher level of accuracy and reset expectations with the customer based on that level of accuracy.

LEAN AIs

The process above, called Lean AI, is intended to build a small but complete AI to solve a specific problem. The process can help new companies and established outfits alike, turning them into AI-First companies.

The goals of building a lean start-up are different from building a Lean AI. Instead of trying to start a company, you're seeking to complete a project for an existing company. Instead of trying to get a product out the door, you are attempting to make your model accurate. Instead of having product features as milestones, your milestones are model features. The output is a prediction, not a calculation. The performance and function of the prediction in the customer's workflow are less important than the accuracy and reliability. The table below illustrates the different milestones.

MILESTONES FOR LEAN START-UPS VERSUS LEAN AIs

LEAN START-UP	LEAN AI
Minimum viable product	Minimum predictive accuracy
Product features	Model features
Output a calculation	Output a prediction
Performant	Accurate
Functional	Reliable
Product usage	Prediction acceptance
Launch a company	Launch an AI-First product

Building a lean start-up is different from building a Lean AI. Instead of building a product and a company, you're generating a prediction and a system. Instead of showing a demo, you're showing a report. Feedback is not qualitative (whether the product is easy to use) but quantitative (whether the prediction was accurate enough). The table below shows the differences at each step of the process.

BUILDING LEAN START-UPS VERSUS LEAN AIs

STEP	LEAN START-UP	LEAN AI
0	Understand the customer's problem	
1	Determine product features	Determine model features
2	Build a product	Generate a prediction
3	Show a demo	Show a report
4	Receive qualitative feedback	Receive quantitative feedback
5	Build more features	Collect more data
6	Relaunch the product	Retrain the model
7	Measure usage	Measure accuracy
8	Launch a company	Launch an AI-First product

PUTting MVPs Aside

The lean start-up popularized the concept of a *minimum viable product*, or *MVP*: the minimum set of product features a customer needs for a product to be useful. The reason to define this set of features is to optimize the amount of time spent building a product before showing and selling it to customers. That is, to not waste time building things that customers are unlikely to want.

This book, *The AI-First Company*, uses the concept of *prediction usability threshold (PUT)*: the point at which a prediction becomes useful to a customer. That threshold may be at the point where the prediction starts getting better than a human's. However, sometimes a prediction is usable even if it's less accurate than what a human can make because it may be more consistent coming from a computer. Remember, a "prediction" in the world of AI can mean a classification—for example, classifying what type of bridge is in a photo. The reason to define this threshold is to optimize the amount of time spent building and tuning the models that generate predictions before showing and selling them to customers. That is, to not waste time getting data and building model features that don't make the prediction more useful to a customer.

The PUT is nuanced and specific to a customer. Most models don't require 100 percent accuracy to be useful. Sometimes, where the model is used to make a critical decision, the PUT will be very high. Figuring out when, how, and for what purpose a customer needs a particular prediction helps to nail down the PUT. Ideally, at this stage, the PUT, customer ROI, and POC metrics are linked.

Redefining Features

Product features are analogous to model features. Features in the discipline of product development are software functions that help a user output a calculation. Features in the discipline of ML are a set of mathematical functions that are fed data to output a prediction. Product features are said to be performant—able to reach a calculation fast—in the way that model features are referred to as predictive, or capable of making accurate predictions. Product features determine what a customer can do with a product. Model features determine what a customer can predict with a model.

Features need to be fed data, perform lots of calculations, and be fine-tuned by experienced ML engineers. Collecting data, computation, and ML engineers are expensive. Thus, it's prudent to spend time figuring out what customers specifically want to predict in order to settle on the features that will get to the PUT. Capturing the training data, training a model to the PUT, testing it on real-world data, capturing feedback data, measuring ROI, and delivering it to the customer in a useful package all come after defining features.

Finding Features

There's one more step to Lean AI that's just beyond the statistics work above: developing the first models. This usually starts with running simple algorithms over some customer data to generate a prediction, even if it is low accuracy, or below the PUT. Finding features for these initial models can involve the following:

- talking to customers or other domain experts to get ideas for causal factors;

- building an interface that allows customers to override the prediction when it doesn't make sense;

- setting up a regression to see if some data correlates with other data;

- clustering to see if there are trends in the data, or to create smaller clusters on which to build models;

- running a random forest algorithm over it to see if random decision rules lead to a plausible conclusion; or

- repurposing a model trained on a similar dataset or exploring transfer learning, a technique to apply models trained on one dataset to another (keeping in mind that this can be difficult and costly to implement).

Presenting the results of this feature-finding process to customers may yield feedback that can inform how to structure the next experiment.

CONCLUSION:
LEVELS TO LEAN

Messing about with ML frameworks for months may mean never getting a product out the door. Taking a step back, one straightforward approach that I've seen work well is to speak to potential customers and distill what they say into a few problems to solve with statistics. Messing about with technical frameworks is fun, but I hope that the business frameworks in this chapter are just as much fun as you venture into new problem spaces in the hope of finding solutions that form the basis of a whole new product—and a whole new business.

The following diagram shows the path to building AIs the lean way. The bottom rectangle indicates the degree of vertical integration to bear in mind while working with customers. Capture just enough data to train the model to test in real life, capture feedback, measure ROI, and package the model into something that will convince customers to take the next step with you.

Starting small with statistics is a safe bet. But you're here to build an AI-First company, not a data science consulting shop. You build an AI-First company by using the Lean-AI process to understand your customers' problems, picking one and delivering a stand-alone solution. Lean AI is the process of trying to make predictions from a small sample of data, then presenting those to contained groups of stakeholders to figure out their expectations of a feature-complete product. Starting with the Lean-AI process is like tasting a bite of pie before eating the whole thing—for you and your customer. Delivering a product using the Lean-AI process lets you get fast feedback before taking on higher customer expectations, harder modeling challenges, and more data. With Lean AI, anyone can get started on the path to building an AI-First company.

THE LEAN-AI STACK

Anti-Lean AI Startup

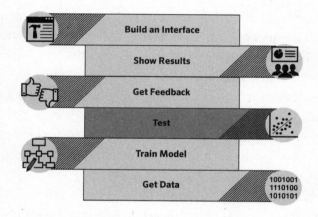

Lean AI Startup

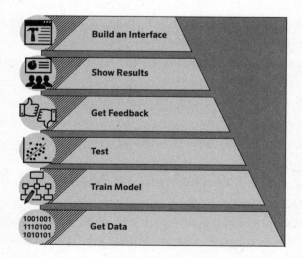

PLAYBOOK

- **The first thing to build may not be AI.** Customers may need both non-AI and AI-based methods.

- **Start with statistics.** Get one answer, with one statistical method, then use that to discover the next answer using another statistical method. Many AIs are built on features discovered in experimental data science.

- **Start with a single question.** Starting with one question zeroes in on one dataset, reducing the need to wrestle with poor data from multiple databases.

- **Start with a single algorithm.** This reduces the chance of the solution breaking.

- **POCs prove accuracy.** AI-First products tend to require a proof of concept phase because the value proposition of the product is the prediction. Potential customers need to know whether that prediction is accurate when made for them—on their data and in their environment.

- **Lean AI is a process to build an AI-First product.** The process is about solving a specific problem with AI and building a small but complete AI that can grow into other domains or remain focused on one.

- **Lean AI is not the same process as the lean start-up process.** The goals of building a lean start-up are also different when building an AI the lean way. Instead of building an MVP, get to the PUT. Instead of product features as milestones, model features are milestones. The output is a prediction, not a calculation. The performance and function of the pre-

(continued)

diction in the customer's workflow are less important than the accuracy and reliability.

- **Different types of customers demand different levels of accuracy.** Each customer has a threshold at which a prediction is usable in their business: the prediction usability threshold.

- **Reframe features.** Features in the discipline of product development are software functions that help a user execute a task: to output a calculation. Features in the discipline of machine learning are a set of mathematical functions that are fed data to output a prediction. Product features are said to be performant (to calculate fast) in the way that model features are said to be predictive (to predict accurately). Product features determine what a customer can do with a product, whereas model features determine what a customer can predict with a model.

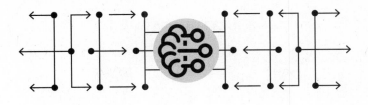

THREE

GETTING THE DATA

All companies function to generate a return on assets, and AI-First companies are no different: they generate income from data. Getting data is the first step to take toward building a DLE.

> data learning effects = economies of scale to data + data processing capabilities + data network effects.

The amount of data in the world increased dramatically in the second decade of the twenty-first century as billions of devices connected to the Internet. There seems to be an imperative to vacuum up data, but there's limited capital to acquire data. Data can be a valuable asset on a stand-alone basis, but it can also kick off a DLE. AI-First companies put capital, time, and effort behind getting data, ahead of other strategic priorities. But how to procure unique data? Where does a data strategy begin? This chapter covers methods to value data in order to smartly scope data acquisition projects, where to look for data, and how to create it from scratch.

GETTING DATA

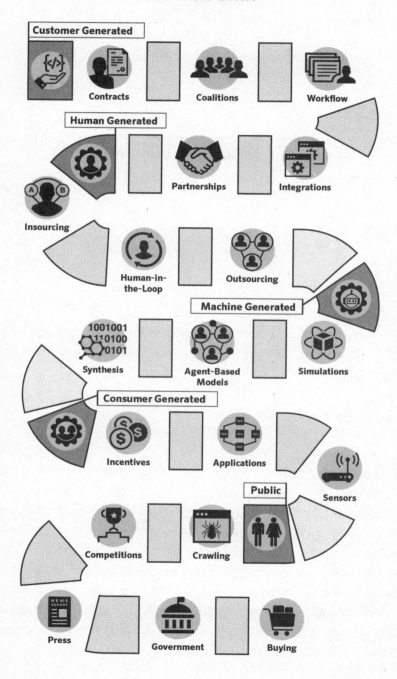

Customer Generated

Contracts · Coalitions · Workflow

Human Generated

Insourcing · Partnerships · Integrations · Human-in-the-Loop · Outsourcing

Machine Generated

Synthesis · Agent-Based Models · Simulations

Consumer Generated

Incentives · Applications · Sensors

Public

Competitions · Crawling · Press · Government · Buying

VALUATION

Before investing in data acquisition, establish a framework for valuing data.

**DISCRIMINATION—
WAS IT HARD TO GET?**

❑ Accessibility

❑ Availability

❑ Cost

❑ Time

❑ Fungibility

**DETERMINATION—
IS IT USEFUL?**

❑ Perishability

❑ Veracity

❑ Dimensionality

❑ Breadth

❑ Self-reinforcement

Discrimination

There are five ways to value data based on how difficult it is for others to get it (as opposed to its ultimate utility to the acquirer of that data): accessibility, availability, cost, time, and fungibility.

Accessibility

Data that is hard to obtain might be hard for others to get, too. To give you an example, it might require traveling to a special site, such as a local council office, manually collecting paper files, photocopying them, and then running them through *optical character recognition software* that turns the image from the photocopier into text that a computer can read. It's important to assess whether data may be hard to obtain in the future, based on contracts or policies related to a dataset. Typically, this might involve the data owner's restricting access to it. For example, both government agencies and private vendors often make data publicly available at no cost for a set period of time before beginning to charge for access or deleting it from circulation.

Availability

The time it takes to pull data from a given system presents a barrier to others. Some systems only allow harvesting data at a very slow rate, perhaps because it is costly to run the system from which to pull data or to stratify data products based on different rate limits. One example is financial market data, where market data providers allow access to stock price quotations only during certain, relatively long intervals (usually microseconds) unless the customer pays more to pull it in shorter intervals. Paying more for the more frequently available data can give that customer a competitive advantage if they use that data to make important decisions, for example that difference of a few microseconds may allow an AI-First trading system to make a profitable trade over its competitors.

Cost

The price charged by data vendors is an obvious barrier. That price is sometimes clearly stated by the vendor in dollar terms but sometimes less clearly stated, in the form of revenue sharing arrangements with the data vendor or by requiring the purchase of expensive software to access the data. For example, a terminal provided by Bloomberg, the New York–based financial data and media company, costs thousands of dollars per month to lease, when it is just a relatively basic computer made of commodity components. However, it provides access to high-quality, real-time data on financial markets. The price of data can sometimes be paid in nonmonetary forms, such as submitting some internal data before getting access to the vendor's data. Given that not all data is of equal value to everyone, it can be hard to assess the exact cost of the contributed data. However, the assessment of whether that data contribution requirement presents a barrier to competitors can be based on the minimum amount of data required to contribute, its format, the completeness of each row, etc. The more strict the requirements, the more difficult it is for competitors to contribute and thus access data from the vendor.

Time

The time it takes to collect data can give a head start over competitors that may want to collect that same data. Some data can be amassed at a certain rate: for instance, weather data dictated by the revolutions of the sun, and employment data dictated by the rate at which the relevant government bureaus assemble it and make it available. Therefore, anyone wanting to obtain a critical mass of that data released in such a way simply needs to collect it for a long time.

Fungibility

The *fungibility*, or interchangeability, of data affects whether data presents a barrier to others achieving the same goal with that data. Data that is fungible can be swapped out for different data (that may be cheaper) without negatively affecting the quality of the decision made based on that data. For example, you could use text from any news website to train a model to understand the general meaning of a sentence model.

Determination

There are also five ways to value data based on its ultimate utility (as opposed to how hard it is for others to acquire): perishability, veracity, dimensionality, breadth, and self-reinforcement. This is less straightforward because it depends on the intended use of the data.

Perishability

The rate at which data perishes determines relevance. Old data may no longer represent reality and thus can cause models to generate an invalid prediction. For example, the price of stocks changes almost instantaneously, so the price from even just a second ago isn't as relevant as the price from a microsecond ago (depending on which features the AI-First trading model uses to make a prediction about stock prices). Other data types have long shelf lives: mapping data that includes the height of Mount Everest will not change (much) and thus will remain relevant for many years. Then there are cases in between, such as consumer preference data taken from surveys. Sometimes preferences are long lasting, such as clothing sizes, and sometimes they are not, like styles that may be in fashion for just a season.

Perishability can be mitigated by updating. The rate at which the vendor or source updates the data affects its perishability. Sometimes data vendors will stratify their pricing on the updating rate, charging more for more recent data. Perishable data is generally less valuable because it needs to be updated constantly, and this either costs money for computing the operations on that data or for fetching more data.

Veracity

The veracity of data determines reliability in the context of making a decision. Often, determining veracity requires manually validating data points: for example, getting a sample of product specification data such as the voltage of a power supply—just a few rows—and checking it against data manually collected from the manufacturer. Sometimes data vendors help to determine the veracity of data by adding a guarantee that it's accurate. Finally, there are third parties that verify data accuracy across a suite of vendors by industry or on a bespoke basis.

Dimensionality

The number of dimensions in the data determines whether it's relevant to making a decision. Dimensions are attributes of a given entity. Typically, this manifests in the number of columns in a table of data. For example, demographic data can include age, gender, income, and more.

Dimensionality is a particularly powerful determinant of value; the intended use is training an ML model because each dimension informs the model when it's trying to learn shapes and patterns in the data.

Breadth

The breadth of data determines how closely it represents reality. Breadth is the number of entities or points on a distribution. This is typically manifested in the number of rows in a table of data. Breadth means more examples of the same type, and more variations in the attributes of entities and edge cases. Sometimes more breadth comes through joining datasets from different sources or vendors, but this requires them having the same attributes. Often, combining different datasets by lining up the attributes and filling in any missing data gets more breadth.

Self-reinforcement

Self-reinforcing data becomes more valuable over time. Self-reinforcement manifests in attributes of the same entity that change over time but are measured in the same way. For example, performance feedback on an employee is represented as one value at one point in time and another at a later date, but the later value reinforces the worth of the first value. This is because if the two data points are the same or trending the same way, they reinforce the value of each other.

The Volume Question

Many people are concerned with acquiring large volumes of data and often trade off getting more data for getting better data. What's more important depends on the type of decision to make and which models may help to make that decision—whether using human or machine intelligence. For example, training a model to recognize something in an image may require a few hundred images if they are labeled but a few hundred thousand if they are not labeled, because different image recognition systems require different amounts of examples and labels. In the world of understanding natural language, the most advanced model at the time of this writing used 499 billion tokens; the one that preceded it, just over a year earlier, used 10 billion tokens. However, models to recognize specific clauses in a legal contract can be trained on a hundred Word documents. And these numbers will change in the months after you read this book, thanks to developments in the field of AI. The returns to scale on data are rarely linear, depending on the decision to make and the models used to make it.

DATA VOLUME AND VALUE

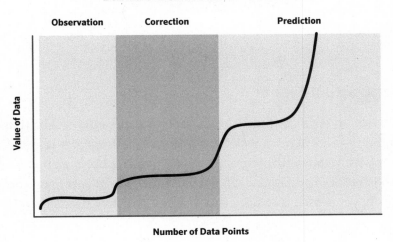

CUSTOMER-GENERATED DATA

Perhaps the most significant source of data for AI-First companies is from the customers they're serving. AI-First companies are, after all, building products to predict something of commercial or industrial consequence for those customers, so it makes sense that the predictive models are based on those customers' data.

CUSTOMER GENERATED

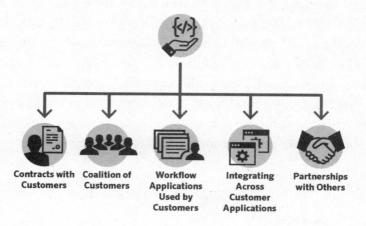

| Contracts with Customers | Coalition of Customers | Workflow Applications Used by Customers | Integrating Across Customer Applications | Partnerships with Others |

Contractual Rights

This section will outline some strategies for negotiating data rights and give tactical advice on how to structure contracts to build a competitive advantage through data. This is an opportunity to establish robust protection against incumbents and emerging copycats beyond what traditional intellectual property strategies offer.

The Clean Start Advantage

At the dawn of the "cloud era," in the 2000s, the vast majority of large companies were hesitant to entrust their data to an outside party. For many of them, it was the first time they'd been asked to store their data offsite. To assuage these concerns, cloud computing vendors would often explicitly forgo all rights to the customer data they managed. Many of those agreements are still in place, hampering cloud era companies in their attempts to build intelligent systems. They must now face the challenge of renegotiating data rights with their existing customers or go on an acquisition spree to get data.

Today's AI-First companies, however, can approach customers who are more comfortable letting third parties manage their data, enabling them to engage in a different conversation about the data. AI-First companies are seen as less established and well positioned— and thus less competitive—than the big cloud vendors, and so they are better positioned to negotiate data rights successfully.

Negotiating

Negotiating data rights with customers is a chicken-and-egg problem. Leverage comes from demonstrating good results, but AI-First products need data in order to achieve those results. AI-First companies solve this problem by finding alternative sources of data through the following methods:

- targeting small and medium-sized business customers with more open attitudes toward data rights or data that's perceived to be of relatively low value, perhaps explicitly trading off data rights for reduced prices;

- providing a free version of the product that liberally captures data but has limited functionality; or

- selling an ancillary product at cost in order to capture the data.

Many of these external data sources can be sufficient to train models to the PUT of business customers.

Structuring

The following is an all too common story: a start-up approaches a large company with an incredible demo of a new AI-First product that promises to automate a tedious task. The customer agrees to a pilot with the intent to buy. Unfortunately, the contract gets stuck in the legal and compliance departments: no way will they give the start-up access to their data, lest it be mishandled or fall into the hands of the competition. The start-up is dead in the water.

AI-First companies get ahead of potential compliance concerns by making it clear from the outset of negotiations that their main interest is in learning from data and the *data exhaust*, such as user engagement and interaction data, metadata, and data flow information. Here we'll outline a few ways to formulate contracts to get rights to customers' data, with the following goals:

- make models better—and thus products more useful for customers—over time by adding new, machine-learned features;

- adapt models to customers' changing conditions;

- prevent competitors from reaching similar levels of efficacy; and

- own a valuable asset.

The tactics for achieving these goals incorporate the following concepts, which ultimately are worked into the contract.

- **Models.** These are the models used to make predictions about something specific to a particular customer. It could be something built for that customer based on their needs, fine-tuning specific features, or something that was built for all customers and then modified to the data from that customer so that the output of the model, given the same data, will differ from one customer to the next. Essentially, a model (in this context) is something that is not useful *across* customers.

- **Global, multiuser models.** These models make predictions about something common to all customers. These are generally trained on data aggregated across all customers and include features that were designed to work across all customers. Essentially, a global model is something that is useful *across* customers.

- **Data.** This is the customer data. This data is not processed in any way at all. This data is often proprietary to customers.

- **Anonymized and aggregated data.** This is the data referred to above but processed in some way so that it cannot be referred back to a particular customer. Anonymize data by *hashing* it, removing data points that can be linked directly to a particular person, *pseudonymizing* data, *randomizing*, or *redacting*. Anonymized data can be aggregated across customers to train models general to all of those customers. This aggregation process will take one data point of a certain type that's common across all customers and then put all of the data points of that type in one table: say, the number of times a product, as identified by a Universal Product Code (UPC) from a bar-code scanner, was scanned on a particular day across all customers.

- **Personally identifiable information.** Some data is classified as *personally identifiable information (PII)* and thus carries certain legal obligations in the United States as well as other countries. This data may need to be handled in a certain way to comply with regulations. Some customers just will not grant access to that data because they are ultimately responsible for any mishandling of PII.

- **Storage.** Data can be stored in the public cloud or on privately owned servers. Customers may want different types of data and models stored in different places. This may be outlined in the contract.

Flipping some of the concepts above, here are some contractual terms to avoid:

- customers owning global, multiuser models;

- restrictions on using anonymized, aggregated data across customers to train those global models;

- liabilities for managing PII;

- fracturing data architecture by having to store data in different locations.

Customer Data Coalitions

Customer data coalitions are a single company (the vendor) organizing a group of companies (the customers) to share data with one another. Data coalitions often create a unique data asset for both vendors and customers. Using a common framework, here is why customer data coalitions build good data assets.

- Smaller companies often don't have *enough* data to train and run intelligent systems. This means that they are more prone to problems such as *overfitting*, where the model thinks that a particular data point is representative of the feature it is trying to predict, when, in fact, that data point is an outlier. Having a greater volume of data enables customers to effectively average across many data points when training their systems.

- Members can see different variations of the same *category* of data from other members. For example, images of a product taken in different lighting conditions used to train computer vision models to recognize the product in different environments.

- Members can *validate* data points for each other. For example, if they have a user with the same (not personally identifiable) data in some dimension—email, let's say—but not others, such as a preference for liquid or powder detergent, they can correct those other data points by unifying on the email address and filling out the "detergent preference" column for the user with that email address.

- Some companies collect data on a consistent basis, perhaps streaming from a device or point-of-sale system. Other companies collect data on a periodic basis—say, from quarterly surveys or whenever they happen to buy data. Data from some members of the coalition can help other members that are having a slower season adapt to what's currently working.

Building a data coalition is as simple—and as difficult—as requiring that every customer agree to share their data with every other customer. This is effected in the contract by granting the right to use the data in certain ways, such as to train an ML model. Data can be anonymized and aggregated differently—segmented so that customers don't share all of their data, and so on—depending on what customers want to contribute and access by joining the coalition. There are a few challenges with building customer data coalitions.

- **Marketing.** Getting coalition members to team up against a behemoth can be powerful but requires inspiration. Potential members will have some of the same hesitation that any company has with sharing data. Think about picking initial members based on their relative competitive position, size, and sophistication. The right messaging can bring those companies together.

- **Contracts.** The contract between the vendor and every company that joins the coalition has to be the same; no special deals where some customers have access to some data and some don't.

- **Anonymization.** This can be of particular concern in customer data coalitions because these customers may ultimately compete against one another, often directly.

Let's consider what a data coalition trying to compete against Amazon would look like. Most purchases start with search and most product searches happen on Amazon. The search functionality and recommendations on its website help consumers quickly find the products they want to buy not only because the thousands of engineers working on search and product discovery in earnest since 2003 built a good product but also because Amazon has a lot of data on what consumers want to see in search results. This data allows the engineers to train high-accuracy, machine learned models that power suggestions in the search bar, the ordering of results, and product recommendations on various pages. This makes for a high-quality search experience that produces relevant suggestions. It also makes competing against Amazon difficult. Other e-commerce retailers are unlikely to have either the engineering or data resources that Amazon has and are thus unlikely to create the same high-quality experience. One could start a coalition to change the game by letting retailers use both highly engineered product discovery products and data aggregated over all of their customers. The coalition of retailers contributing data coupled with training a machine learned system on that data could yield more accurate suggestions, results, and recommendations than any one retailer could achieve itself. This allows any member of the coalition to compete with Amazon. Collective intelligence comes to the fore yet again.

Workflow Applications

This common alternative to obtaining data from customers works especially well with smaller customers, because they tend to be less sensitive about sharing data.

A *workflow application* is a piece of software that takes a sequence of things that someone does in the real world and puts those steps into software. An example would be taking a list of tasks from a project manager on a construction site—currently written down on a piece of paper—and inputting them into a mobile application so that he can track those tasks, assign them, and generate a report. Workflow apps are all around us. Indeed, we're still in the era of building such workflow apps for many industries—a huge opportunity for software developers willing to learn how specific industries get things done.

Workflow products gather data. Each piece of data entered into a workflow app goes into a database. By way of example, let's consider car insurance claim processing. First, the assessor goes out to the damaged vehicle sitting in the body shop, takes some photos of it, and writes a report. That report is sent to a *loss* adjuster at the insurance company so that she can decide whether to pay for repairing or replacing the car, and for how much. Sometimes the customer will disagree with the assessment, so the whole process is repeated. These steps currently happen with pen, paper, clipboards, faxes, and cameras. A far better solution would be a single app that takes the photo, has text fields for the report, and automatically sends the report to a queue for the loss adjuster to process. Disputed claims can be kicked back to the assessor for reassessment if necessary. This data on what type of damage should be repaired or replaced, how much it will cost to repair, what cars are valued in what way, etc., is most valuable and very hard to gather.

Business process data goes in and out of workflow apps all day, every day. Companies can use this data to build an intelligent system—that is, a system that goes beyond recording work to automating work by predicting a next step, and even automatically filling out parts of a form. Continuing the example above, imagine an application that enters the car's specifications; determines from photo files the extent of the damage; and calculates the total cost. This would automate many of the more tedious aspects of the assessor's job, cutting down on travel and either auditing or replacing the loss adjuster's work. The result of collecting data and then building an intelligent system is smarter workflow products.

The San Francisco software company Expensify started out offering a better way to manage expenses simply through improved integration with banks and credit card providers. The product pulled transactions from these services and then put the transactions into expense reports. Dragging and dropping expenses into reports was a much-improved experience over manually logging each one. Expensify's second act was to build an artificial intelligence-based product that automatically categorized expenses. This system trained with all of the data from the core workflow app that allowed customers to link transactions to categories, tags, and reports.

This ability to take a real-world workflow, develop software around it, and then add further data and features is why I believe that all business software will one day be intelligent.

Integrators

Data integration products can passively assemble large volumes of data. These products attract customers because they make it easy to link one data source to another, normalize it across sources, and update the integrations as the connections to the sources change. Data integration companies such as MuleSoft and Informatica dominate the market for products that perform such functions, and that market is growing as more data is stored in a multitude of different applications and made available through *application programming interfaces (API)*. Data *integrators* build a valuable data asset by directly collecting data that flows through their pipeline or by generating metadata based on usage patterns, derivations, or other observations.

However, building a company based on integrations is difficult for the following reasons.

- Basic forms of data integration are easy to replicate, and the need for data integration is well known, so there are lots of companies in this market.

- Cloud computing companies have a strategic imperative to offer a product that pulls in data from a multitude of sources so that they can charge more for storing more data.

- Data pipelines break for unforeseeable reasons that are specific to sources, and fixing them can involve a great deal of manual work. This heavy, unforeseen work can cost a lot, reducing gross margins.

- Pricing power tends to be low because purchasing a product to integrate data is typically a decision made after the purchase of another product that's solving the core problem. Thus, customers tend to have less of their budget left when they get around to purchasing the integration product, or they just go with whatever data integration the vendor of the core product recommends.

That said, Mulesoft went all the way to an initial public offering (IPO) with this strategy, and the companies Segment.io and Zapier successfully executed data acquisition strategies centered around tools that integrate a multitude of data sources. Segment, acquired by the public company Twilio for over three billion dollars, unifies marketing data across different SaaS products and internal databases. Its API-driven approach started with a simple, catchall analytics product, Connections, which competed against Web analytics products in the first act by getting data from the following sources:

- mobile apps through Apple iOS and Google Android;

- Web apps through its Analytics.js plugin, Shopify, and Word-Press;

- servers (directly); and

- many cloud apps, from CRMs, to payment, to email apps.

This data pipes into email systems, analytics dashboards, help-desk apps, marketing attribution tools, and data warehouses. The second act saw Segment use the data it acquired through customers to build an intelligent system that automatically unifies user history across data sources into one comprehensive profile with an associated, intelligently generated user persona; synthesizes data into traits, audiences, and predictions for each customer; and then uses these enrichments to personalize marketing campaigns and in-app experiences.

Segment's first act was collecting data by integrating many existing data sources; the second act, building an intelligent system that undergirds an AI-First product with this data.

Comparison

Building a workflow app is a very different task from building integrations. Here's a comparison between workflow-first companies and integrations-first companies.

WORKFLOW-FIRST	INTEGRATIONS-FIRST
Collect data from what humans see	Collect data from what machines do
Analytics on static data	Machine learning on streaming data
Reactive/post hoc	Proactive/real time
Threatening to data originators/ other workflow apps	Neutrally positioned with respect to workflow apps

Integrations-first apps have some advantages over workflow-first apps if the goal is to develop a data asset. Perhaps the most significant of these is that integrators gather voluminous, fresh (that is, closer to real time), and structured data directly from machines. These machines can include software applications; this doesn't just mean data from sensors. Higher data volume, freshness, and consistency of structure generally lead to higher-quality predictions.

Integrating data that comes from workflow apps can be user-input data that may be inaccurate, unstructured (text, for example), or out of date. Accurate data means better models and more accurate predictions.

That said, integrations-first approaches can be more difficult than workflow-first approaches. First, data from integrated services is generally not proprietary data, unless those services are internal to a company. Second, the available data depends on the data structure of the workflow app. Contrast this with a workflow-first approach, accumulating specific data points by adding *user-interface (UI)* elements or forms in the workflow app to collect data from customers.

Partnerships

Forming partnerships with other companies is a way to obtain lots of data for little money. Partnerships tend to most easily form when the partners have *complementary* data. Data is complementary when it increases the value of existing data. For example, data on income is complementary to data on debt if you're looking to build a credit model. Two companies, one with data on income and one with data on debt, could benefit from sharing data if one of them is building a model to predict creditworthiness and the other is building a model to predict consumer spending. Both companies have an incentive to share data because each of their models improves with the additional data.

Complementarity of business models is also a consideration. Companies that make money in different ways are more likely to want to set up a data partnership because any gains they make won't be competed away by their partner's gains or by marketing them to the same customer base.

This is distinct from being a data integrator. Integrators collate data from their customers through a set of integrations with other products, but only if that fulfills a specific customer need and goes through existing pipes between the customer's data storage and the application to be integrated. This also means that vendors don't have to negotiate deals with each of those external data sources.

For instance, computer vision offers a promising path to helping physicians identify diseased tissues such as cancers of the skin, breast, lung, and so on. However, computer vision models tend to need many images on which to train, and there are strict controls on handling patient data such as X-rays. Companies building computer vision–based systems need that data but can't get it without either running their own medical facilities—which would take years to build and approve—or obtaining it from an existing medical facility. Thus, AI-First companies—big and small—set up exclusive partnerships with medical facilities. The AI-First companies need a critical mass of data to train the model to the PUT. This can give them an advantage over others in the market.

On the customer side, medical facilities want increased accuracy, reliability, and efficiency for each diagnosis. Sometimes the priority is avoiding missed diagnoses, in the case of particularly deadly cancers such as lung cancer, while in others it's about cost-effectively screening lots of patients on a regular basis, in the case of particularly prevalent cancers like basal cell carcinoma of the skin. Medical facilities achieve this by using AI to augment the physicians on staff but don't typically have the ML computer vision expertise to build AI. They have a valuable asset to leverage as well as protect, so they typically strike partnerships that give them exclusive access to the AI product for a period of time, include strict controls on data, and allow for integration into existing hardware such as X-ray machines. The exclusive access could give them a cost advantage or allow them to market improved accuracy and reliability to potential patients.

The company building the AI can work with the medical facility to get a critical mass of labeled data, get their models to the PUT, figure out how best to deliver the prediction through existing hardware, work through regulatory issues, and receive feedback from physicians in the field—all things the medical facility couldn't do alone. The second phase could be a gradual expansion of the partnership to associated facilities, or a broad market release, sharing the revenue from new customers for a period of time. The AI-First company brings the models, the customer brings the data, and their business models are complementary.

HUMAN-GENERATED DATA

Employ people to build highly specific datasets, whether through outsourcing, hiring people, or having existing employees use products that generate data.

HUMAN GENERATED

| Insourced Labeling | Human-in-the-Loop Products | Outsourced Labeling |

Data Labeling

Many ML models require labeled data for training recognition algorithms. There are some promising transfer and semisupervised learning techniques that may provide alternatives to gathering a great deal of labeled data, especially for generic domains such as image, video, and language understanding. However, the state of the art doesn't seem to offer enough just yet, and particularly not for specific domains. Accessing and owning processed data to feed models can be the single hardest problem in starting a vertical, AI-First business.

Supervised ML models need labeled data. Getting lots of labeled examples for specific domains is hard. For example, where would you find a hundred thousand images of 2001 Chevy Silverado fenders? Crowdsourcing, running surveys, or building a tool for car mechanics is not likely to yield that many images in short order. You'd probably have to procure such data from a company that has been photographing cars for years, like a car manufacturer, a chain of body shops, or an insurance company.

In the absence of existing labeled datasets, build one. This entails building a team to label data, which may include both experts and nonexperts, and requires tools to efficiently label large volumes of data.

There is a burgeoning area of management practices for managing teams of data labelers. When given clear goals, data labeling is a highly measurable activity. For example, if the goal is to get a model to an expert level of accuracy, start by having experts label each observation; then move to having a machine label some, with a nonexpert correcting those labels. The goal is to have the machine plus a nonexpert agree with the expert—hence the metric of expert-nonexpert agreement rate.

EXPERT LABELS AND PERFORMANCE

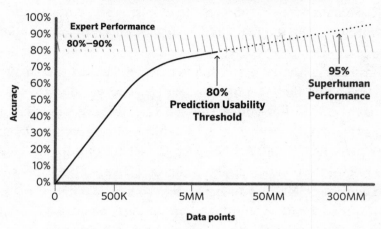

Over time, the economic value of a particular data labeling operation can be quantified in terms of money saved by automation over the cost of each label, multiplied by the number of labels required to get the model to that level of automation. Articulated another way, the *return on investment (ROI)* in hiring people to label data equals the savings from automation over the cost of people required to be in the loop of the ML system to keep it at that level of automation.

> ROI of labeling operation = (Money saved through automation/Cost of each label) * # labels.

Perhaps it's helpful to think of this operation as a factory. The "good" it produces is labeled data. The factory manager's job is to find efficiencies along the production line.

Tools

Labeling often requires engineers to clean data before applying the labels. For example, it is very hard for a machine to learn patterns across the text in millions of customer service emails. In this case, an engineer may use a natural language processing technique—an area of ML focused on understanding text—to locate the segments of these emails where customers mention specific products, then she will cluster the text to build up categories of complaints about those products.

These categories are then used to label all the new emails that come in so that the machine can learn how to respond to complaints in different categories. Humans can label every email that comes in with these labels, or the machine can guess which label to apply to which email. The former approach is expensive and the latter often inaccurate. Techniques such as active learning are useful to find the emails for which a human label would help the system improve the most, and thus find the right balance between manual and automated labeling of each incremental email.

THE ACTIVE LEARNING PROCESS*

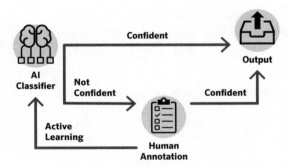

For example, in the case of labeling images, the system presents a cluster of images and asks the labeler to group similar images. An active learning–based model reviews what is similar about the images lassoed by the user, groups them together, and asks the labeler for more information about the images in the smaller cluster. The

---

* Lukas Biewald, "Active Learning and Human-in-the-Loop," SlideShare, last modified June 30, 2016, https://www.slideshare.net/crowdflower/active-learning-and -humanintheloop-63622196. Edited by the author.

labeler then groups similar images into a bunch of subclusters, and the model learns what is similar about the images in each subcluster, and so on. Essentially, the active learning model predicts what data it needs next based on which of its last predictions the labeler identified as accurate.

THE ACTIVE LEARNING INTERFACE*

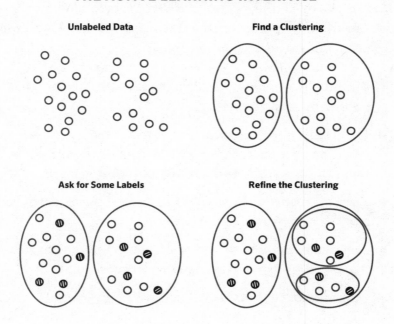

Active learning–based systems are hard to build but valuable. First, people without technical skills can create extremely useful labels by giving feedback to a system. Second, the system can be most helpful in domains where the range of possible solutions to the ML problem is so wide that navigating the solution space would be very expensive in terms of time and cost of computation. People

---

* Sanjoy Dasgupta and Daniel Hsu, "Hierarchical Sampling for Active Learning," in *ICML '08: Proceedings of the 25th International Conference on Machine Learning* (New York: Association for Computing Machinery, 2008): 208–15.

can contribute shortcuts on this navigation by quickly having the machine mutate the output to be more like the end goal. However, there is a question around influence: Do the machine's suggestions influence the user to the point that the user starts labeling data in a way that they think will just agree with the machine? If so, the labels won't be useful.

Thinking of users as data labelers can be particularly powerful; for example, by adding prompts asking users to label pictures. Some algorithmic approaches may help to pinpoint the most useful data to procure from users.

- *Uncertainty sampling.* Labeling those points for which the current model is least certain.

- *Query by committee.* Train many models on the same labeled data. Then have people manually label the data points that caused the most disagreement in output between the models.

- *Expected model change.* Have people label the data that is most likely to change the model's output.

- *Expected error reduction.* As above but focused on the data that would most likely reduce the model's error.

- *Variance reduction.* As above but minimizing variance.

This is not an exhaustive list; there are a variety of other approaches based on the fundamental concepts of ML.

Interactive machine learning (IML) is the field of creating such interfaces that collect data to train a specific ML model and then present the results back to the user so that they can make a decision about which data to put into the model for its next iteration. IML can be thought of as yet another way to have teams of *paying users* label data rather than *paid employees*.

On the development side, IML can allow for faster iterations when building classifiers. Traditionally, engineers will develop classifiers based on information gathered from conversations with users. When users are correcting—and effectively training the classifiers—iterations are faster. For example, engineers building a system to automatically write marketing emails can usually come up with a few of their own examples of representative emails or find a set online. However, generating some samples and putting them in front of marketers using a product that manages email campaigns elicits more salient feedback on what makes a good or bad marketing email.

The potential downside of having machines learn from humans in this iterative way is that the people may feed the machine uninformative examples. This could overwhelm the machine to the point of its classifier becoming inaccurate. Developers, however, can put safeguards in place to prevent users from flooding the machine with unhelpful examples. Simple methods include having multiple users label the same data point, or running an alternative, noninteractive model alongside the interactive model and then comparing results in order to note where the interactive model conflicts or ignores the noninteractive model.

One benefit of developing an IML system is that asking for user input builds trust. Allowing users to "correct" the output of a system and then see that their corrections affected the system's next output promotes trust in a number of ways. First, users will be able to explain—to themselves or others—how the system works, at least in part, because they've seen it take an input and compute an output. Second, the system will accord with users' opinions—formed objectively or otherwise—on what the output should be. Finally, users have seen some causes of their effects: some output from their input.

Best Practices for Building Data Labeling Operations

Setting up a team to label data can be a core process advantage for an AI-First company. Before assembling a team, however, consider the large, platform-based solutions for labeling such as Amazon's Mechanical Turk. These platforms have many workers, from all around the world, who are able to cope with highly elastic demands and can label data twenty-four hours per day. They also provide tools to assist workers so as to keep costs low and quality high.

Management

Individual labelers are hired depending on the required expertise, and the labeling team can be split between experts and nonexperts—the expert labelers having some experience in classifying the data on hand. These individual labelers generally report up to a labeling manager. Naturally, the number of individuals reporting to a labeling manager depends on the degree of supervision required. Where there are multiple labeling managers, they could report up to a head of labeling. This head of labeling, or sole labeling manager, reports to a vice president of operations in a midsized company or directly to the chief operations officer (COO) in a smaller company. This may be different when the labeling operation is nascent and still trying to figure out what and how to label, in which case it may be more appropriate to report to the head of ML research or the chief technology officer (CTO).

A rule of thumb is one labeling manager for every fifty to a hundred labelers in environments where the labeling isn't completely automated. Again, this depends on the mix of expert to nonexpert labelers.

The cost of a labeling operation hinges on the number of labels required, along with the difficulty of acquiring them, the leverage gained through labeling tools, and the degree of expertise required to label. The cost can range from a few cents per label, using Amazon Mechanical Turk, to hundreds of dollars per label, using a doctor.

Nonexpert labelers can be recruited from a variety of places, given the minimal experience required in the role. Classified ads or hourly work agencies are a good place to start. Another option could be to recruit directly from labor marketplaces such as Amazon Mechanical Turk or the freelancing platform Upwork. Expert labelers, on the other hand, will be recruited directly from their respective fields: for instance, radiologists from radiology clinics or loss adjusters from car insurance companies.

Labeling managers often come from an operations background—that is, a role where they had to coordinate lots of resources, given cost and time constraints. Motivating and managing lower-paid workers could be a requirement where the bulk of labelers on the team are of the nonexpert type. An example of a good background for a labeling manager would be having managed call center operations.

Measurement

The ultimate goal is a good product, and a good product is based on accurate classifiers. Thus, a key metric should be whether the classifiers are getting more accurate.

Quantity has a quality of its own in ML. In other words, a large quantity of labels can increase the accuracy of a classifier even if any one of those labels isn't necessarily correct. A large volume of labeled data can also be an asset itself. Thus, tracking the total labeled data points can be informative of the value produced by the labeling operation.

Labels aren't free, and business models need to balance the revenue that comes from producing a good product with the cost of delivering it. Cost per label is an obvious measure to track. Perhaps less obvious is the fact that it's good to track because it can indicate how much leverage comes from tools to help labelers, and the required expert/nonexpert mix of labelers.

Consensus among labelers about a given data point can be a sign of label accuracy because a lack of consensus means the measure of accuracy may be wrong. Experts are more likely to label data more accurately than nonexperts. Track the accuracy of nonexperts' labels by their rate of agreement with experts' labels. Experts also cost more than nonexperts, so gradually modify the ratio more in favor of the nonexperts to reduce costs. The model's output should agree with customers' real-world data over time; that is, predictions should accord with reality. If this agreement rate drops, there may be a problem with data labeling.

Human-in-the-Loop Systems

Human-in-the-loop (HIL) systems require human input to generate an output. These systems don't necessarily have active or interactive learning—they could just have people labeling data that goes

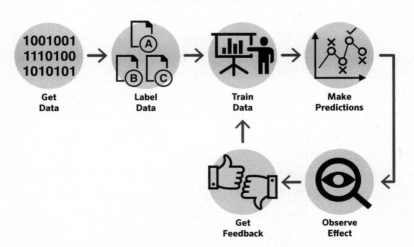

HUMAN-IN-THE-LOOP SYSTEMS

Get Data → Label Data → Train Data → Make Predictions

Get Feedback ← Observe Effect

in a bucket somewhere. Similarly, active and interactive learning systems don't necessarily have humans in the loop—it could be a robot doing the labeling. HIL systems are the general form of getting users to label data.

The loop is the preceding diagram. Typically, there are a few different ways to get humans in the loop.

1. **Creating.** Ask them to create brand-new data in the "get data" step; for instance, by completing surveys.

2. **Labeling.** Label data either by entering text or picking from a list of labels used by the ML system.

3. **Feedback.** Score the output, using either a binary score such as true/untrue or correct/incorrect, or a scalar score such as ranking from 0 to 10.

Outsourcing

Data labeling can be supercharged by an IML system and putting humans in the loop. The choice depends on the degree of expertise required to label the essential data, the availability of experts, the cost, and the potential for increasing automation over time (and thus how the cost of labeling data affects profit margins). Sometimes, however, outsourcing data labeling completely will be the best option.

The biggest reason to outsource is to get more labels. Getting correct labels is a function of expertise: labelers experienced at recognizing certain objects are better at doing so. However, *all* labelers will label objects incorrectly *some* of the time. The way around this is to have more labelers so that the incorrect labels are effectively diluted by the correct labels. Mathematically, if a labeler makes a mistake 5 percent of the time, the probability that three labelers make the same mistake is 5 percent × 5 percent × 5 percent, or just 0.01 percent.

Outsourced or crowdsourced workers both create and label data. They can collect data in a multitude of ways: for example, by calling people, completing online searches, copying information manually from a website, and other methods that can be reduced to a standard, discrete, short task. They label data using the interface provided to them by the marketplace to both add labels and track their work. Some marketplaces have a human-in-the-loop system to label data. Workers can also be effective at cleaning data, whether by de-duplicating lists of data, correcting spelling errors in lists of text, or discarding blurry images.

The trade-off of outsourcing is less specialization. Outsourced operations aim to cater to a broad range of customers, and so they have labelers for all sorts of content, from movie characters to cars on a street. These labelers are not trained to recognize specific objects, such as a particular model of car or *perturbations* in a glass structure. However, outsourced operations can be cheaper than insourced operations, thanks to the tools they build for their labelers or the rates they negotiated with workers. Companies tend to experiment with both *insourcing* and outsourcing, achieving a balance over time, depending on their labeling needs.

Outsourcing can take many forms. There are consulting firms, business process outsourcing firms, and others that will create custom labeling operations with associated expenses and margin for them. On the other hand, there is a burgeoning crowdsourcing industry in which individuals work for a small fee on a per-task basis. The aforementioned Mechanical Turk and Upwork are examples of marketplaces for task-based labor.

MACHINE-GENERATED DATA

Machines can consistently, quickly, and cheaply generate data for models, either as a complement to human-generated data or a stand-alone resource.

MACHINE GENERATED

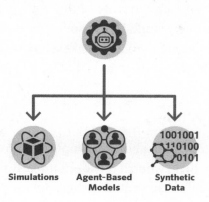

Simulations   Agent-Based   Synthetic
Models   Data

Simulation

Software engineers use *simulation* to verify the functional correctness of a program, such as simulating all the ways through a maze in a videogame or how electrons will flow through a circuit board. Simulations test software. Programs contain logical rules, written by humans, but we can't always imagine all of the possible inputs to a program, so we write simulations to generate those inputs, then put those inputs through the program and see if it fails.

As we moved into the AI era, software engineers found another use for simulation. AIs contain models, made up of features, written by humans or machines. These features change the function of the software—without further design work—as they learn from inputs. This is the point of difference: simulations find failures in normal software but find improvements in AIs.

Simulations thus present a significant opportunity to improve AIs, particularly *reinforcement learning* and other, *agent-based learning AIs*. Such models typically need to try multiple approaches, and, since existing datasets are insufficient or unavailable, simulators are useful. The models have a goal from the designer of the model and an environment in which they can try lots of different approaches to achieving that goal—a simulator—that incorporates the constraints of the real world in which the model must ultimately work. If the model achieves the goal in the simulated environment, then it can take what it learned into a production setting, making predictions that lead to real decisions.

Agent-Based Models

How do we generate data about a complex environment? It's easy to model what y will do when it responds linearly to x. However, it's very hard to model what y will do when the function or even the number of variables is unknown. Complex economic and biological systems have many variables and flow-on effects to every action. Modeling the behavior of individual agents at the microlevel of every decision can help us understand what may happen elsewhere in the system at a macrolevel. Understanding breaking points, path dependency, and other critical factors in a system allows for a better appreciation of their potential consequences. This is possible with *agent-based models (ABMs)*.

ABMs model the behavior of agents, given a set of incentives and environmental constraints, with respect to other agents. This field draws on disciplines such as game theory, sociology, complexity, evolution, and randomness. Creating an ABM requires figuring out how many agents are in the system, how they make decisions, how they learn from their actions, and how those actions affect the actions of others in the system. Agents follow programmed rules. Sometimes programming an agent requires expertise in a specific domain—understanding the "rules of the game," or the principles of the system. Programmers create ABMs using techniques such as adversarial and reinforcement learning. Popular agent-based systems include some that play John Conway's Game of Life and solve the prisoner's dilemma.

Financial and political institutions often use ABMs. For example, the Bank of England uses ABMs to model the impact of policy on property and credit markets. The effects of mergers and acquisitions on competition can be modeled effectively using simulation. Macroeconomic forecasting using agent-based models is of interest to traders and market makers at hedge funds, banks, and asset managers. And ABMs are also used by governments to assess the potential effects of environmental policies.

ABMs aren't the same as simulations. Think of agent-based learning as a superset of simulation: ABM environments are loosely defined, whereas simulation environments are strictly defined. Another way to view the difference is that ABMs learn about behavior, while simulators test for specific outcomes.

Synthetic Data

Brand-new data can be synthesized by devising a set of rules that output data points. These rules can be created in a prescriptive way—for example, all tables must have four legs—or they can be learned from an existing dataset, such as getting a model to recognize that all chairs also have four legs. Synthesized data maintains the structure, concepts, types, and dependencies of the existing dataset. The difference between synthesis and simulation is that simulation is used to verify, whereas synthesis is a process of creation.

There are many uses for synthetic data. Engineers who want to test a new product feature on customer data often use real customer data. This can lead to mistaken manipulation of live customer data or unauthorized viewing. Salespeople who want to demo a functioning product often can't do so without the data underlying the product. Often, they will just demo the product with barely obfuscated customer data, potentially exposing customer information to competitors. Beyond both of these situations, any handling of live customer data can result in a mistake that leads to a security breach. The safest option is not to use customer data for anything at all.

Synthetic data can be particularly useful in certain scenarios where labeling data is unfeasible, either because of cost or difficulty, as shown below. Most of the examples used relate to images and computer vision models, but the dimensions apply to other types of data.

- **Scalability**

    Labeling objects of a certain form—a chair, for instance—is feasible because most humans can recognize basic objects. However, objects are slightly different when one considers all the potential variations within the form, such as a lounge chair, a dining chair, an office chair, etc. Training a model to recognize chairs means recognizing all types of chairs, so the training data has to include representations of all types of chairs. Getting images of all types of chairs and people to label them will be expensive to the point of being unfeasible—even more so when one considers the different types of materials used to manufacture a chair, covers that can obfuscate a chair, and so forth. Synthetic data generators can take the basic components of a chair—legs, covering, back or no back, etc.—then run through all the variations and combinations of those components to generate thousands of examples for a very low cost.

- **Flexibility**

    Labeling objects from one perspective is feasible because most of those objects will look the same from a certain perspective—say, looking at a house from the street. However, objects are slightly different when one considers them from different perspectives—from high above, for instance. Training a model to recognize objects from any perspective is necessary if the source of ongoing data will be a camera that moves around, like that on a drone. However, accumulating a multitude of perspectives on the same object effectively multiplies the cost of data acquisition by the number of perspectives. Synthetic data generators take a single object and offer unlimited perspectives by, for example, modeling the object in 3-D and then moving around it, generating a labeled data point at each step.

- **Accessibility**

  Labeling objects is often feasible because pictures of them are readily available, as with cars on a street. However, some objects are simply hard to find, such as pictures of tanks in an active war zone. Getting the data to train such a model could be prohibitively expensive or practically impossible. Synthetic data generators can take a hand-built model of such an object and drop it into various environments. Building such a generator can be expensive, but the cost can be amortized over all labeled data points because the one generator is used to produce many examples of the same object. These generators are typically built using the same tools that videogame designers use to build game environments.

- **Probability**

  Labeling objects is often feasible because they occur fairly regularly, as in the case of a wave breaking on the shore. However, some objects are rarely seen in the real world, such as explosions caused by lightning. Getting the data to train such a model is often impossible without lots of historical footage or waiting a very long time. Synthetic data generators can take a scenario and produce it on demand.

- **Cost**

  Synthetic data may be cheaper than human labeling because a program that generates lots of images may be run on computers at a low, marginal cost. However, this is not always the case—for example, where generating synthetic images requires 3-D models that have to be either purchased or drawn by experienced computer graphics artists.

- **Speed**

  Synthetic data can be faster than human labeling. Labeling processes that involve packaging the data to be labeled, sending it to a labeler, waiting for them to do the job, checking, sometimes redoing the label, sending it back, retraining the model using that incremental label, etc., take time. Synthetic data generators can almost instantly generate data to be incorporated into a data pipeline right away.

Synthetic data is thus useful for generating unstructured data such as images, but less useful for generating structured data such as user information. Synthesizing images of chairs with multiple dimensions would be relevant to lots of different customers because chairs often appear in our shared world. However, synthesizing data representative of a particular group of users would *not* be relevant to lots of different customers because those users don't have the same profile across customers. Synthesizing data for a single use case is one task that requires one program. Synthesizing data for many use cases is only one task that requires one program if those use cases have a shared reality, such as the physical world.

CONSUMER DATA

Consumers may contribute data when properly incentivized. This is different from customer-contributed data, the difference being that customers pay for the AI-First product, whereas consumers just take the output of a product.

CONSUMER GENERATED

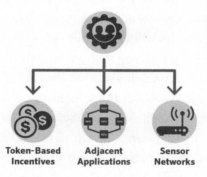

Token-Based Incentives   Adjacent Applications   Sensor Networks

Token-Based Incentives

Blockchain-based ownership tokens, or crypto tokens, can be used to incentivize people to submit data to a network. Given that these tokens are relatively new, it's worth defining some terms.

Blockchain: a decentralized and distributed public ledger of transactions.

Crypto token: a representation of an asset that is kept on a blockchain.

Data network: a set of data that is built by a group of otherwise unrelated entities rather than a single entity.

The idea is to issue a crypto token to a group of people, they submit data to a data network, that data is sold, and the revenue is then distributed back to the owners of the tokens.

The blockchain offers two benefits in building a data network. First, blockchains can verify the provenance of data. The data gets a unique identifier upon submission that is recorded by every entity on the blockchain. When someone has a question about when, or even whether, that data was submitted, query the blockchain. Provenance is all but guaranteed where the blockchain has a sufficiently large number of entities verifying transactions. Second, crypto tokens are a way to securely and automatically pay data contributors. Calculating payments is strictly mathematical and transparent. Token owners get paid according to their contributions of data to the network, verified by all entities on the blockchain. Tokens are verified by a decentralized set of entities, meaning that no one party can invalidate a token owner's claim to payment. Token management systems are scalable for two reasons: one, because, once registered, ownership doesn't need to be changed or managed, and two, payments are automatically calculated based on a formula depending on the contribution, reducing the potential for conflict between the system operator and contributors.

The challenge of running a data network on the blockchain is standardization via validation—that is, automatic compensation for contributions requires automatic verification upon submission. Standardization makes this possible by compensating only contributions with specific parameters, such as a name and an email address. Where parameters are hard to specify, software-based validation upon submission might allow different forms of the same type of data as long as it passes a filter that includes ranges for certain values.

Consumer Apps

Consumer apps were perhaps the most significant source of unique data for the current leaders in the technology industry. Facebook built a competitive advantage through data and compounded that with ML. These companies vacuum up large volumes of data from their users on a daily basis, then use that data to make predictions that improve the consumer products or the business models around them.

Google brought some of the most innovative products to market over the last couple of decades, and they don't charge consumers for many of them. The company has, over many product initiatives, taken the approach of giving away products for free to collect data and gain market share. Then it uses this data to build systems that predict which ads people want to see, and sell those predictions in the form of well-priced, high-performing ads to brands. The link between the data-gathering activities on the consumer side and the revenue-generating activities on the business side is obvious today, but not when Google started. At the time, most advertising on the Web was in the form of banners—essentially online billboards not targeted to any particular visitor to a website. Google changed this paradigm in a few ways, mainly by basing predictions on what visitors to their website were searching and other, ancillary data, such as each person's location. This data proved to be incredibly effective at increasing the rate of interest visitors take in the ads and thus how much money Google makes from selling these ads.

Google provides us with many other examples of a sound data strategy. Google Translate is free, but Google doesn't sell the lexicon it is developing as users make translations. TensorFlow, an ML model management tool, is free, but Google doesn't sell the data that people are feeding its models. Google Search is free, but Google doesn't (directly) sell search data to marketers or other search companies. Google is a durable business because it has consistently pursued a strategy of collecting valuable data to build intelligent products.

Facebook brought us all closer in the world's dominant social network, and it doesn't charge consumers for anything. The company's products amass an enormous amount of data as users share their interests, hopes, and dreams with friends—and the company continues to release products that collect more of this data. Facebook uses the data to build systems that predict which ads people want to see and then sells those predictions in the form of well-priced, high-performing ads to brands. Facebook's ads are particularly effective because its visitors are logged in while browsing Facebook, meaning that Facebook knows them on a one-to-one basis and thus can target ads to them more accurately.

Amazon changed how to get stuff, making it cheaper and easier to do so than through any other means, for many categories of products. The e-commerce behemoth collects data about what customers want based on what they buy and how they browse, then uses this data to make better recommendations. Amazon has been doing this for so long that the company can make better recommendations than other shopping websites.

Harvesting data from consumers for one reason then selling it to corporations for a different reason is common and can be the basis of a big business. 23andMe did this with genomics, BillGuard with purchasing data, Credit Karma with credit scoring, Onavo with app performance, and Dark Sky with location data. However, building a durable business this way can be difficult. First, the "trick" that gets users to submit their data may not last; another company could utilize the same trick or come up with a different trick to get the same data while charging less. Second, the trick may involve paying out money to data conduits (for instance, paying developers to install a *software development kit*, or SDK, to be the data pipeline), and profit from selling the data may disintegrate if those developers want to charge more or customers pay less. Third, one can't capture value and earn revenue on a recurring basis from static data because that data provides value to customers only at a point in time before decaying.

Incidentally, it's worth making a point of the corollary: the current leaders in the technology industry are not business software companies. Companies are hesitant to give other companies their data. Large business software customers typically operate in competitive industries and so restrict what they share with any outside software vendor that may also sell software to their competitors. Consumers, on the other hand, don't have such competitive considerations to make and, in any case, haven't been as concerned with privacy.

Sensor Networks

Compiling data from the real world—rather than just from other bits of software—involves a different set of considerations. Creating a network of sensors to collect data is a way to build a defensible dataset because deploying such a network can be costly. Think of a sensor as anything from a simple counting device to something more complex, like a black box on an airplane.

The most obvious and available *sensor network* is that of the world's mobile phones. These phones have many individual sensors in them that can be utilized by software applications to collect data. For example, the app Dark Sky gets atmospheric pressure data from the barometric sensor in phones and aggregates it to provide ultra local weather predictions. It also happens that the company is gathering location data that it can sell to third parties. Most of the data from sensors in a phone are captured by companies today, but there may exist an opportunity to collect unique data from relatively new sensors or by working with sensors in a different way.

The next most obvious and available sensor data is from commodity sensors, which are cheap and abundant. Given their cost and availability, such sensors would not, of course, generate proprietary data out of the box. The proprietary data, in this case, would be generated from a network of such sensors. The competitive advantage is generated here through proprietary means of distributing the sensors—for example, placing a device in every retail store in a particular region to count the number of people who enter and exit.

The least obvious and least available source of sensor data is proprietary. One could build sensors to measure anything from biological signals and bodily functions to an undersea phenomenon such as a thermocline. However, building and manufacturing sensors can be hard, depending on their complexity. The design of the sensor, as well as the materials used to build it, the componentry to connect the sensor to a computation device, the communication methods, the production process, and the integrations with existing sensors—all can be sources of competitive advantage by way of legally protecting the intellectual property. Once built, there is the challenge of getting people to install sensors. People won't install a beeping, power-hungry device in their home without some commensurate benefit. The most obvious incentive is to pay someone, like the Nielsen media ratings company pays people to install a box on top of their TV that tracks their viewing habits. The next, most obvious incentive is to provide an application on top of the data coming out of the sensor that helps the user in some way. Another successful model has been to offer savings to sensor users: for instance, installing power use sensors, collecting the data, aggregating it across the network of sensor users, and then negotiating savings with the power utility.

PUBLIC DATA

There are many public sources of data available to AI-First companies. Such data can be hard to access and wrangle but is often free.

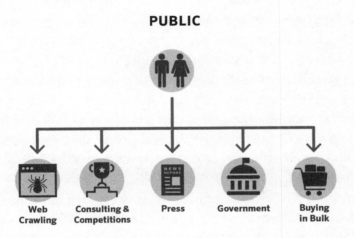

PUBLIC

Web Crawling | Consulting & Competitions | Press | Government | Buying in Bulk

Crawling

There is a lot of information on the Internet. Much of this is structured and could thus be used to train ML systems. This is how Google gained a data advantage, and the company arguably runs the world's biggest *Web crawler* today.

Quantity has a quality all its own, in that accumulating a significant amount of data can be a competitive advantage. Amassing data from the Internet is usually referred to as *crawling*. Typically, a *crawler* is a program that systematically looks up Web pages or other resources on the Internet through a URL, strips out the unnecessary content on those pages, such as formatting, grabs the salient (or all) data, puts it in a standard document format (for instance, JSON), and delivers it to a private data repository. For example, the crawler could go to the website of the US Securities and Exchange Commission (SEC), the government's financial markets regulation division, access company reports stored there as HTML (*hypertext markup language*) files, strip out the formatting, find annual revenue numbers, put those in a JSON document, and then store them in a database. Crawling can be technically difficult because Web pages and other resources are always changing in form, location, and availability. Good crawlers need to adapt.

Crawling is a big business, and many companies offer crawling as a service. Some build a custom crawler that gathers data points from specific resources. Some regularly pick out fresh data from a specific set of Web pages, using crawlers that were built to adapt if the pages are not available or change. Others offer customizable crawling systems that can extract whatever data is available on the Web pages.

An alternative to a crawling service is to use an application programming interface that offers data as a service (DaaS). This service effectively does the crawling then offers up data through specific endpoints in an API. The companies providing data as a service run their own crawlers—and perhaps other data collection methods—on a constant basis to offer current, high-quality data that is readily available. Other features might include feeding an email address into an API that returns the name, title, and company where a person works. The company offering the service can source this data hundreds of different ways, such as crawling public sources and government websites.

Crawled data isn't proprietary because others can access it on the open Internet. However, processing this data—"cleaning" it—can effectively transform it into proprietary data and make it useful to those building ML models. Usually this means structuring the data so that it has some numerical value that can be computed by a probabilistic system.

Consulting and Competitions

Some companies have loads of data and a big problem to solve but no way to use the data because machine learning is hard. This creates an opportunity for data seekers with ML talent to be matched up with those who have data but no ML talent.

The simplest manifestation of this strategy is to set up a consulting project with a data-rich company, making sure to maintain the right to keep the data (or some version of it) after completing the project. Such projects can take the form of highly customized data science work.

A more advanced manifestation of this idea is to build a platform where companies submit datasets and problems, then a community of people submits ML models that solve the problem to a sufficient degree of accuracy. The company that pioneered this idea was Kaggle, an online community of data science and ML practitioners, founded in 2010. Data scientists and ML engineers can go to Kaggle and browse datasets, which they use to build models for solving a prediction problem. Many times, the person or group that submits the most accurate prediction wins a cash prize.

There is potential to create such a platform but in a distributed way, so that anyone can contribute to any dataset on a platform and then run it anywhere without anyone seeing the data or the models. This would enable companies with valuable, private data to have data scientists and ML engineers around the world build predictive models based on that data without ever seeing it—no risk of private data breaches. On the other side, data scientists and ML engineers could create valuable models without letting people see exactly how they constructed them.

The components of such a system that allows ML on private data involve concepts such as *federated learning, differential privacy, secure multiparty computation*, and marketplace incentive mechanisms like blockchain. In such a system, data owners submit data or a basic model with a bounty for training the model to a certain degree of accuracy. Then the model is encrypted and uploaded to a network—public or private—of ML engineers. Upon completion of the training, a reward would be issued, depending on the accuracy achieved. The ML engineer can then choose whether to decrypt the model with his or her private key for the party that issued the bounty. At no point in this process would either party have access to each other's data or intellectual property in the form of ML algorithms and models.

Data-Driven Media

Press can kick off data collection. This is an indirect method—not built into a product—but an effective way to collect data. Articles in the media, whether print or online, can generate participation by compelling readers to contribute data to the author, such as an article ranking all the companies in an industry by the number of successful projects. Readers in that industry want to be ranked highly on the list, but the publisher needs details on their projects to properly rank the company. So, the reader submits data. The publisher then updates the rankings and now has valuable data. This is a form of enlightened self-interest, in that the data submitted by the companies helps not only the publisher but the company as well.

Governments

Governments were traditionally the largest systematic collector of data through the census. Thanks to the work of President Barack Obama's White House, some of the US government's data is available in a structured, accessible form through APIs.* The Obama administration required government agencies to make public data

---

* "API.DATA.GOV," Data.gov, accessed September 11, 2020, https://api.data.gov.

available through such APIs so that individuals could not only access public information in a more systematic way but also try to build useful applications with government data.

However, this data isn't proprietary and thus is not a source of competitive advantage. What will be a source of competitive advantage is data that is manually or digitally collected from public sources in a way that hasn't been done before. This could be anything from manually transcribing government records, to securing onsite access to an offline government database from which to extract data. Such opportunities to get public data that is otherwise not easily available exist particularly at the municipal level of government because those lower levels of government typically do not have the resources to create and maintain online resources for their constituents.

Buying Data

We've left the most obvious source for last: buying data in bulk. There are many companies out there that sell data, from public companies specializing in selling consumer data, to gimmicky apps that capture data through Facebook and sell it on the side. Companies sell lists of people with addictions to alcohol, sex, and gambling, and those desperate to get out of debt. The world of data brokers is odd.

What Do Data Brokers Do?

Data brokers acquire a critical mass of data of a specific type or about a specific subject, put it in the one place, and perform useful operations on the data such as cleaning, basic analysis, and enrichment with complementary data. Brokers may sell insights rather than just the data. Sometimes the broker owns all of the data it sells; sometimes it owns some and licenses some. However, to the end customer, the data is packaged and priced, with the broker handling any licensing issues.

Brokerage is challenging because, while customers are strictly "renting" data, they often get the value up front and have no reason to come back for more data later. The key, for data brokers, is to sell data that needs to be refreshed at regular intervals, such as stock prices.

Data brokers typically make data available through an API, from which the customer requests certain data points and receives them in a structured format. The data is often piped into other applications such as marketing automation tools. This is often referred to as data as a service (DaaS) because the data is served to the application rather than received in bulk.

Breaking Down the Brokers

Marketing data brokers typically sell profiles of individuals so that brands, political parties, and other entities can target them directly. These profiles aren't always identifiable as a person. Rather, they are a set of attributes tied to an identifier. This identifier can be a name, an email address, or just a pseudonymous identifier, and the accompanying attributes range from basic (for instance, age), to personal (an answer to a survey twelve years before), to abstract (clicks on banners).

There are also companies that create derivative profiles on top of these attributes, such as psychographic or demographic profiles, and put individuals in different buckets, depending on their inferred preferences, tastes, or other factors. Essentially (and pejoratively), these are models that systematically stereotype people to make it easier for marketers to direct campaigns most suitable for certain groups.

Financial data brokers aggregate financial and company data. The most elementary of such data is *ticker data*—that is, stock prices with a time stamp. Investors also want data they can use to build valuation models of companies, such as lists of companies in a given industry, financial statement information (public and private), product lists, consumer surveys, and historical consensus valuations. Bloomberg is just one company in this market that earns more than $10 billion in revenue per year.

There are many data brokers in other verticals. Companies can buy medical data, industry-specific data, product data, and more.

The Brokering Process

Buying data from an established data broker is generally straightforward. A pricing sheet outlines the cost per data point, charged upon refreshing the data through an API or other medium. The process may be more complicated with a smaller broker, involving forms to fill out and USB sticks sent through the mail. Then there's the option of negotiating a deal to buy bulk data in a one-off purchase from someone who has a particular dataset.

The following checklist may be useful when buying data:

❑ **Verification.** Did someone—a third party or the broker itself—verify the data as accurate? If not, you may end up with junk.

❑ **Structure.** Is the data in a usable format? If not, you may have to spend money reformatting it before ingesting it into your data pipeline.

❑ **Ownership.** Does the broker own the data being sold? If not, you may have someone chase you down to get back his or her data or to litigate.

❑ **Compliance.** Was the broker compliant with relevant laws, such as those to protect individuals? If not, you may be at risk of incurring a fine for using the data.

❑ **Security**. Does the broker secure the data being sold? If not, someone may hack the broker, pinch the data, and release it to the public—making the data you bought worth a lot less.

Don't Sell Your Data

AI-First companies may consider whether to sell their data. This is generally a suboptimal way to earn income from a data asset. Data brokers are not valued as highly as companies that utilize data to build a product. Using that data as the basis of a DLE may create more value in the long run.

Let's consider how two very successful companies came to the same conclusion. Facebook and LinkedIn, for example, each realized partway through its lifetime that its data was extremely valuable and consequently cut off access to its data through APIs. They did this to protect their ability to capture the full value of their assets by selling high-value applications: LinkedIn's sales and recruiting products, and Facebook's advertising platform. That would not have been possible had they sold the underlying data (profiles) to other companies capturing value at the application layer.

Accruing a proprietary dataset, while painstaking, is a valuable thing to do. But it's just step one in creating a DLE. Feeding that data into a self-learning software system that produces insights for customers is the next step toward building a durable technology business today.

CONCLUSION:
GET IT HOWEVER YOU CAN

Every week, I seem to hear about yet another novel way to acquire data. The creativity around simply obtaining data is remarkable, let alone the creativity involved in building the next wave of tools for society. Sure, some of these are single-use methods, but stringing them together to amass a valuable dataset is the first step to building an AI-First company that will be competitive for a long time.

When it comes to gathering data, there's no one right way, no golden thread, and there's no exhaustive list; get it however you can. This chapter provided some ideas and a place to start. Approaching data acquisition with the valuation framework at the start of this chapter allows for appropriate allocation of capital when both acquiring and amassing data, and in planning how you'll keep that data fresh. The next chapter shows you how to pick a type of AI based on the data you've got.

PLAYBOOK

- **Discriminate between the value of different datasets.** Physical or legal accessibility, temporal availability, cost, time, and fungibility are useful proxies for whether someone else can get the same data, and thus whether it affords a competitive advantage.

- **Determine the value of data based on its relevance to your use case.** Perishability, veracity, dimensionality, breadth, and self-reinforcement indicate whether a dataset improves predictive accuracy.

(continued)

- **Obtain data from customers.** Thoughtfully construct contracts with customers to balance their ownership of the underlying data with ownership of the AIs trained on that data (including the models and self-generated data).

- **Accumulate data from lots of smaller customers.** Smaller customers may be more willing to share their data, not to mention easier to reach with marketing campaigns in the early stages of product and market development. Larger customers, on the other hand, may demand restrictive terms of use for their data and discounts for contributions.

- **Create a data coalition.** AI-First companies can organize customer data coalitions to beat behemoths.

- **Build workflow software to gather data.** Data about business processes flows in and out of workflow apps all day, every day. AI-First companies can use this data to build an intelligent system that goes beyond recording work to automating it by predicting a next step.

- **Pull data from other software.** Linking, normalizing, and updating data across disparate sources is a valuable service. Collect data directly as part of providing this service, or generate metadata based on usage of such a data pipeline.

- **Partner with companies that have complementary data and business models.** Data is complementary when it increases the value of existing data. Companies have an incentive to share data because their models improve with the additional data.

- **Build a team to manually label data.** This can be outsourced, crowdsourced, or insourced. Insourcing means building a team to label data, which may include both experts and nonexperts, and require tools to efficiently label large volumes of data.

- **Utilize active learning to improve the efficiency of data labeling.** Such tools can leverage experts to get many automatically applied labels from a few manually applied labels.

- **Put users in the learning loop.** Users can label, create, and score data. Achieving the highest level of accuracy often requires getting as close as possible to human understanding, so get people involved.

- **Create agent-based models.** Modeling the incentives, behavior, and constraints of agents, then observing how they interact with one another is one approach to getting data, particularly about complex systems.

- **Create simulations.** Setting up a simulation and letting it run can generate data on unanticipated situations.

- **Synthesize data.** Software can create new labels on different versions, multiple perspectives, difficult-to-access, low-probability, high-cost or low-speed instances of the same object. Synthetic data is often used to generate labels on unstructured data, such as images.

- **Set up incentives for third parties to contribute data.** Token-based incentives are a novel way to incentivize data contributors in a given network because tokens set up both the validation and reward steps.

- **Create a consumer product that collects data.** Creating a separate app, launching a consumer product, and deploy-

(continued)

ing sensors are somewhat costly but targeted ways to harvest data.

- **Crawl publicly available data.** The Web, governments, and data vendors all hold a treasure trove of data. Set up crawlers, competitions, or press campaigns to get it.

- **Don't sell data.** Data brokers are not valued as highly as companies that use data to build a product. Use that data to build a DLE.

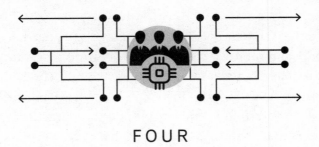

FOUR

AI-FIRST TEAMS

Processing data is the second step to take toward building a DLE.

> data learning effects = economies of scale to data + data processing capabilities + data network effects.

Processing data and moving from a Lean-AI product to a complete, AI-First product requires an AI-First team. This chapter covers who to hire, where to find them, how to support them, the type of management that works best, and how to structure an organization around them. Such people are in high demand, given the potential of AI, and developing a nuanced appreciation of what they do leads to looking for them in places that others ignore, beyond the halls of top computer science schools and into a multitude of disciplines. The challenge down the road is building an AI-First organization, so we cover that last. That requires putting people who can build AI throughout an organization, diffusing knowledge between disciplines.

In this chapter, we will focus on building the teams that process data and build models, covering the different tasks, tools, and training required in order to craft job descriptions. This isn't a book to teach engineers how to build models but to teach business managers how to win. To that end, we propose best practices for placing these roles in your organization so that they're well managed, resourced, and accepted.

WHO TO HIRE

Different technologies require different competencies, and the technology stack utilized by AI-First companies is distinct from that of software companies. AI-First companies utilize high-volume data infrastructure, high-speed query engines, high-concurrency analytics pipelines, computationally intensive visualization products, and ML models. They build interfaces that show the predictions in context and gather feedback. The competencies required to manage this technology are captured by titles such as data infrastructure engineer, data engineer, and ML researcher. AI-First companies may eventually need a team replete with people in all such roles.

The competencies that tend to get bundled into such roles include the following.

- *Data analyst:* set up dashboards, visualize data, and interpret model outputs.

- *Data scientist:* set up and run experiments.

- *Data engineer:* clean data, create automated data management tools, maintain the data catalogue, consolidate data assets, incorporate new data sources, maintain data pipelines, and set up links to external data sources.

- *Machine learning engineer:* implement, train, monitor, and fix ML models.

- *Data product manager:* incorporate the data needs of the model with the usability intentions of the product designers and preferences of customers in order to prioritize product features that collect proprietary data.

- *Data infrastructure engineer:* choose the right database, set up databases, move data between databases, manage infrastructure cost, and more.

- *Machine learning researcher:* set up and run experiments.

- *Software engineer:* write the software that delivers the predictions through an interface, application programming interface, API, or other medium.

- *Designer:* design the interfaces, including any interactive elements that get feedback data from customers.

Each of the data and ML-specific roles tend to be filled by people with slightly different educational backgrounds than a traditional software engineer.

- *Data analyst:* master of business administration (MBA) or bachelor-level courses in statistics, econometrics, economics, mathematics, and other sciences.

- *Data scientist:* higher-level courses in statistics, mathematics, physics.

- *Data engineer:* computer science studies with a specialization in databases.

- *Machine learning engineer:* computer science studies and master-level studies in machine learning, mathematics, or physics.

- *Data product manager:* software product management and design management or project management.

- *Data infrastructure engineer:* higher-level computer science studies with a specialization in distributed systems.

- *Machine learning researcher:* master- and doctorate-level studies in machine learning, mathematics, physics, or computational neuroscience.

WHEN TO HIRE

Sequencing hires carefully helps to manage a company's capital commitment to its data strategy, ability to absorb lessons, and the cultural impact of going AI-First.

The following sequence assumes starting without any data science capabilities and a preference for a smaller initial investment over a larger one. Some companies may have existing capabilities or well-scoped projects that warrant a larger initial investment. AI-First companies, at some point, hire a complete team.

- *Data analyst:* first, because the business need for improving decision-making informs the prioritization of predictive modeling projects.

- *Data scientist:* second, because trying to make predictions with statistical and ML methods provides the initial evidence to support further investment in specific sources of data and types of models.

- *Data engineer:* third, because getting and processing data comes before building models.

- *Machine learning engineer:* fourth, because building a model that works in the real world requires robust modeling and integration with existing software.

- *Data product manager:* fifth, because designing a product to get feedback on the model's output aids improvement and accumulates proprietary feedback data.

- *Data infrastructure engineer:* sixth, because scaling the working models requires managing large volumes of data, processing it fast, and ensuring quality.

- *Machine learning researcher:* seventh, because finding solutions to edge cases demands going beyond readily available ML frameworks to push the state of the art forward.

A final note: outsourcing is feasible for some of these roles, depending on the product, team, and systems. Discrete pieces of analytical work, with accompanying datasets, lend themselves to being outsourced to individual data analysts or scientists who operate as independent contractors. This works well when the analysis to perform, or the questions to answer, are clear, and the data to find those answers is contained in just a few databases. Further, hiring consultants to set up data pipelines, make sound data infrastructure choices, and implement data storage systems can be an effective way to inquire about and instill best practices. The following decision to outsource data infrastructure engineering depends on the data and computing infrastructure in use. Some cloud computing infrastructure companies offer high automation, high-quality data infrastructure monitoring, and remediation as part of their core offering.

Core ML work is difficult to outsource because models tend to require constant tuning, training, and *monitoring.* Data product managers need consistent interaction with customers and users of the product to understand how to best gather data from them and present predictions in the most convenient, usable way. That makes this role among the most difficult to outsource. Finally, ML researchers tend to be among the most difficult to outsource because finding novel, ML-based solutions to problems tends to take a long time, as they call for extensive exploration of internal data, use of expensive computers, full control over experiments, and a consideration of how the resulting models will be implemented by the ML engineers on the team. That said, extended engagements with a team of people—for example, in a university lab—can work well when trying to solve a problem in their particular areas of expertise or research, and can often be supported by joint funding from institutions. In short, whether the role is appropriate for outsourcing depends on whether it involves constant dialogue with customers and business. This table summarizes who to hire and when to hire them.

ROLE	BACKGROUND	COST	OUTSOURCEABLE?	HIRING SEQUENCE
Data analyst	Business	Low	Yes	First
Data scientist	Statistics	Low	Partially	Second
Data engineer	Databases	Medium	Yes	Third
Machine learning engineer	Computer science	Medium	No	Fourth
Data product manager	Product management	Medium	No	Fifth
Data infrastructure engineer	Distributed systems	High	Partially	Sixth
Machine learning researcher	Machine learning	High	Maybe	Seventh

WHERE TO FIND THEM

Starting with statistics means hiring analysts and data scientists before engineers and ML researchers. Essentially, by decoupling data science and software engineering, hiring can focus on data scientists *without* software engineering experience, thus broadening the pool of candidates to include every discipline in which manipulating data is part of the research process.

One can find analysts and data scientists in the fields of economics, econometrics, accounting, actuarial science, biology, biostatistics, geology, geostatistics, epidemiology, demographics, engineering, and physics because these areas require high levels of mathematics and statistics. For instance, a potential hire with an extensive background in physics is likely to be proficient at handling the fundamental concepts of data analysis.

Within those disciplines, look for people with skills that enable them to explore datasets in many of the ways explained in Chapter 2, "Lean AI." These include the following.

- **Statistics.** Measurement, process control, instrumentation, and modeling.

- **Manipulation.** Modeling, clustering, regression, simulation, and visualization.

- **Operations.** Optimization, yield management, manufacturing engineering, systems, dynamics, forecasting, and decision-making.

- **Learning.** Signal processing, control engineering, statistical mechanics, systems, and many more.

HOW TO SUPPORT THEM

Ultimately, motivated people—data scientists or software engineers—want to work on meaningful problems. Communicating the problem, articulating the significance of the milestones to leadership, prioritizing work to solve that problem, and getting the solution out to customers motivates data scientists to do good work.

Data scientists and ML engineers can't do much without data, so acquiring well-structured data in a timely manner is the primary way to support an AI-First team. This book isn't about the best practices of data management, but such practices can be inferred from our discussion on data collection and managing models.

Giving teams the right tools allows them to do good work. Individual contributors generally have their preferred sets of tools, and new tools come out on a regular basis. There is no universal tool. Below is a table of tools that individual contributors may use to illustrate variety, cost, and functionality:

CATEGORY	COST	EXAMPLES
Integrated development environment	Dollars per month	JupyterLab, Jupyter Notebooks, Google Colaboratory, RStudio, PyCharm, Microsoft Visual Studio, MathWorks MATLAB, and Vim/Emacs/VS Code
Collaboration	Hundreds of dollars per month	Dataiku and Amazon SageMaker
Frameworks	Free	Scikit-learn, Keras, XGBoost, Google TensorFlow, PyTorch, and Apache Spark MLib
Cloud platform	Based on usage	Amazon Web Services, Google Cloud Platform, Microsoft Azure, IBM Cloud, and SAP Cloud Platform

CATEGORY	COST	EXAMPLES
Pretrained models	Free	Various open-source software, Google Cloud Platform, Amazon Rekognition, and Microsoft Azure
AutoML	Free	Google Cloud Platform AutoML, AWS Comprehend & Rekognition, Microsoft AutoML, H2O, and DataRobot
Data labeling	Based on usage	Appen, Labelbox, and SuperAnnotate
Visualization	Hundreds of dollars per month	Tableau, Looker, Domo, and Microsoft Excel
Data preparation	Based on usage	Informatica, Trifacta, Alteryx, Tamr, and Paxata

AI-FIRST MANAGEMENT

AI-First companies might need new types of managers. This table highlights some ways in which the management requirements of people on AI-First teams of data scientists differs from traditional software teams of engineers.

EXAMPLES	SOFTWARE ENGINEERS	DATA SCIENTISTS	ML RESEARCHERS
Output	Features	Insights	Models
Measurement	Steps in waterfall charts	Learning that generates questions	Predictive accuracy
Artifacts	Code	Spreadsheets, graphs, presentations, code, or discussions	Models, features, and data structures

(continued)

EXAMPLES	SOFTWARE ENGINEERS	DATA SCIENTISTS	ML RESEARCHERS
Interaction modality	Specifications	Discussions	Reports on experiments
Tools	Managers choose	Individuals choose	Teams choose
Infrastructure	Shared—organization	Singular	Shared—team
Computing power required	Normal	Medium	High

Generally, engineers and data scientists require different types of management for the following reasons:

- Engineers are managed to specific goals, such as releasing a feature, whereas data scientists are managed to both ask and answer questions, such as why something happens. Managing to goals involves tracking progress toward those goals using methods and metrics such as waterfall charts and lines of code. Managing to ask and answer questions is difficult because the answer isn't known ahead of time, and so the goals are often moving targets.

- Engineers deliver concrete artifacts in code. Data scientists deliver results as numbers in spreadsheets, graphs in presentations, models in code, or discussions in person. Progress can be difficult to measure between different sets of results; there is no right answer because the question keeps changing.

- Engineers need certain tools to get the job done; thus, the toolkit tends to be common across a team, set by the managers. Data scientists may pick different tools, depending on the job they're trying to do, and change those tools as they need to employ different methods.

- Engineers get specifications from customers or product managers, fulfill those requirements, and then deliver the result. Data scientists do not get specifications, and so they require regular meetings to refine the questions customers want answered.

- Engineers write code to run on shared computing resources. Data scientists may not eventually run their models on shared computing resources; instead, they may build models on their own computer.

- The computing resources required to run intelligent systems can be much greater than software code. Data scientists may need a larger budget and ad hoc approval of purchases in order to get the computing resources they need, which may require more executive sponsorship and involvement. Commensurately, they may need tighter controls on utilizing computing resources, given the potentially high cost.

Specifically, the degree of difference in managing engineers and managing data scientists depends on the specific role in the AI-First team.

- *Data infrastructure engineer:* little difference. Managed by those that otherwise manage engineers.

- *Data engineer:* some difference. Managed by those that otherwise manage engineers but may require coordination by those managing a company's data assets, such as a chief data officer.

- *Data analyst:* little difference. Management by analytics or business intelligence leaders, or by a general manager within a business unit.

- *Data scientist:* different. Management by nonanalytics leaders is difficult because the work is more experimental and involves advanced analytical methods. Management by engineering is difficult because most of the work is mathematics rather than engineering. Best managed by those with a quantitative background and experience managing researchers.

- *Machine learning engineer:* different. Management by engineering is required because the role involves programming and running models on shared infrastructure. However, ML engineers require some different ML-specific tools.

- *Machine learning researcher:* very different. Management by engineering is difficult because most of the work is mathematics rather than engineering. Best managed by those with a quantitative background and experience managing researchers alongside data scientists.

THE AI-FIRST ORGANIZATION

Position AI talent where they can learn about real-world problems. Designing an organizational structure that positions the best data science and ML staff close to business units makes it an AI-First company. The choice to make is where to sit on the spectrum of centralized to decentralized.

Centralized AI teams have an executive-level leader, such as a chief data officer, who manages all of the data science, analytics, and ML people in the company. That CDO collaborates with the chief technology officer (CTO) and the chief information officer (CIO) to decide which data infrastructure to use. Requests for data, reports, analytical tools, and predictive models go to this central unit, and the unit decides which requests to fulfill. Companies often choose to centralize at the start of their path to becoming an

AI-First company. The key benefit is centralizing decisions about data infrastructure, pipelines, and projects so that data scientists and ML engineers can collaborate effectively on hard problems. The drawbacks are the reduced speed of making data available to the rest of the company, limited access to resources from the core information technology (IT) budget or team, and lack of knowledge transfer from data scientists to domain experts.

Decentralized AI teams have a business unit leader, such as a general manager, to manage the core product delivered by that unit. Data scientists and ML engineers work on projects for and with others in that business unit who have both domain expertise and consistent access to customers. This can be a key benefit, given that AIs often need *heuristics* from domain experts, data from the real world, and feedback from customers in order to reach a sufficient degree of accuracy and thus utility. The drawbacks can include using shared IT infrastructure that doesn't have the features required to build intelligent systems, fragmentation of data, inability to get complementary data from within the company, limited executive engagement with AI-based projects, and lack of knowledge transfer from domain experts to AI experts.

The middle of the spectrum looks like a combination of the two, with some degree of coordination in hiring AI-First teams, placing them across the organization, setting up data infrastructure, managing data, and deciding on projects to pursue, but ultimately deferring to business unit managers on how to utilize data and ML specialists.

AI-First companies distribute AI talent across their organization, have AIs working behind all of their products, and use AI-enabled computing infrastructure. They also have decentralized data science and ML functions, and an executive team that sets data strategy for the whole company. However, not all companies start as AI-First companies, so different companies may be at different waypoints on this journey.

THE AI-FIRST ORGANIZATION

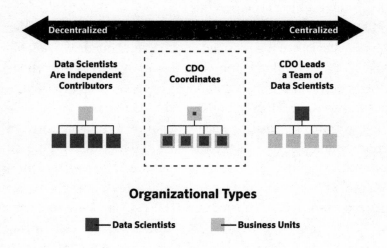

Organizational Types

■—Data Scientists   ■—Business Units

CONCLUSION:
DIFFUSING DATA SCIENCE

The executives I speak to every week—at start-ups and public companies—are all at different points on their way to building AI-First companies, but the difference between those who are moving fast and those who aren't is the mindset: the ones who are constantly integrating the industrial with the technical are building AI-First companies. Embedding AI talent across an organization is a management challenge as hard as any other, but one worth solving in order to be a key figure in the AI-First Century.

Building AI-First teams is at the heart of an AI-First company, but there's no perfect template to follow; no one right way of doing things. There is, however, an approach and methodology by which companies can find suitable candidates, suitably manage them, and structure an organization around them. Developing a fine appreciation of the tasks involved helps to focus recruiting and may go beyond those with just a computer science background. Understanding the work they do helps in managing and supporting them, and ultimately enables embedding them across an organization.

PLAYBOOK

- **AI-First companies need a diverse group of people to manage different technologies.** The competencies required to manage AI technology are captured by titles such as data infrastructure engineer, data engineer, data scientist, data analyst, ML engineer, and ML researcher.

- **AI-First teams need people with different skill sets.** Specialization in databases, statistics, mathematics, physics, econometrics, and economics all help to understand the fundamental principles of AI and run it on modern computing infrastructure.

- **AI-First teams need AI-First tools.** Notebooks, frameworks, cloud services, pretrained models, data labeling, data prep, and visualization tools created for data scientists and machine learners help these teams get the job done.

- **Engineers and data scientists need a different type of manager.** Data scientists ask questions like researchers. They deliver results as numbers in spreadsheets, graphs in presentations, models in code, or discussions in person. They don't get requirements from business users, so they require regular meetings. They may need a larger budget and ad hoc approval of purchases—with commensurate oversight. This is different from a software engineer, who receives clearly specified goals and deliverables from business users.

(continued)

- **AI-First companies put AI everywhere.** AI-First companies distribute AI talent across their organization, have AIs working behind all of their products, use AI-enabled computing infrastructure, decentralize data science, and have an executive team that sets data strategy for the whole company.

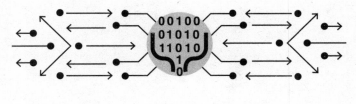

FIVE

MAKING THE MODELS

So far, we have defined competitive advantage, introduced a new and unique form of competitive advantage, showed how to measure it, and given you a blueprint for building it.

data learning effects = economies of scale to data + data processing capabilities + data network effects.

We cover the first part of the DLE equation in Chapter 3, "Getting the Data," and the second part in Chapter 4, "AI-First Teams," Chapter 2, "Lean AI," and Chapter 6, "Managing the Models." Here we cover the last part: how to build data network effects using ML, neural networks, and other techniques that perform operations across a network of data.

Recall the illustration of a data network, copied below.

DATA NETWORK

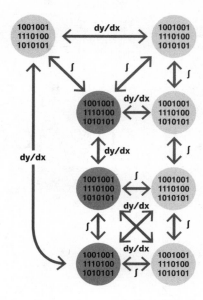

Now we turn our attention to what's happening on those edges (lines). This is all about developing strategies to compound competitive advantage by building ML models.

Breakthroughs in AI happen at a breakneck pace. There are a multitude of ML methods available, many as models ready to apply to data with minimal fine-tuning. What to use and how to tune it depends on the data and the problem to solve, but all of them supercharge learning—increasing intelligence—and some even generate new assets by accumulating unique data. This is why AI-First companies prioritize building these models above other research and development efforts.

Below are some examples of how particular methods generate data. These examples and the accompanying primer serve as a guide for business leaders in their quest to improve understanding of the potential strategic value of ML, not as a guide to making technical decisions.

Primer

Machine learning makes computers intelligent; it enables them to do many things that human beings can do, but at scale, and, as we'll see, many things we cannot do. Developing the ML models requires a lot of up-front human effort. Step one is to correctly frame the problem in terms of an output variable: how many labels to predict and whether to figure out a correlation or classification. Step two: calculate and program the features an ML model can use to identify things. In ML (and statistics), a *feature* is a potential *cause*, and a label is an *output*.

Sometimes one can simply devise some useful features without much help. For example, the pupil of the eye is a small black circle. So, when writing an ML model to identify eyes, one would include a feature that is activated when a given image depicts a geometrically circular, black (hexadecimal value #000000) group of pixels.

Other times, feature engineering requires the involvement of people with expertise in a particular domain. Anyone can identify a pupil, but not everyone can identify a medical malady. Let's use as an example left ventricle hypertrophy, an often silent condition in which the muscular wall of the heart's left pumping chamber gradually hardens, impairing the flow of oxygenated blood to the body. Feature engineering for a model to identify this condition from an image of the heart, taken by an echocardiogram, requires consulting a medical expert who knows which part of the heart is the left ventricle and the wall thickness at which heart function may be impaired. The model can then correlate incoming images with those parameters and flag potential cases of left ventricle hypertrophy. Ultimately, much of ML that is practiced involves correlation, with the domain expert providing and validating hypotheses as to why the correlation might, in fact, be causal.

Furthermore, some things are simply hard to define in machine terms. There are instances in which one can identify the object but not its features, or one can't articulate the features in a way that a machine can generally understand when applying the model to noisy data. For example, I know a zebra when I see it, but I couldn't tell you the typical distance between its black stripes and white stripes. We need to know that distance, though, if we want a machine to recognize zebras. So, we give it a bunch of images of zebras and let it learn that typical distance.

We can supervise a machine's feature learning by giving it a set of data labeled with inputs and outputs. For instance, image x is a zebra, and image y is not a zebra. The machine will then find a set of features that it notices in all the x images and not in the y images—in this case, the typical distance between black and white stripes in the x images.

Machines can also just work their way through unlabeled datasets, completely unsupervised or semi-supervised. The machine will use various methods, programmed by people, to group the data in order to conclude that certain groups are significant features of something.

Here's the approach to defining features when writing supervised ML models:

1. sometimes those features are straightforward enough for anyone to identify;

2. if they are not straightforward, bring in a domain expert to define some features;

3. if they are still not straightforward, write an algorithm to figure out some features by studying labeled elements; or

4. if that's not possible, utilize other methods that don't need features or labels.

A greater number of salient, predictive features make an ML model more accurate, so one will often use all three steps above when developing a model. That said, increasing the number of features increases the likelihood of overfitting the model to the data on which the model trained. As a practitioner, the goal is to increase the number of features that add predictive power, no matter the input data.

Now let's explore the types of ML methods and how each one can create a data network effect, the third component of DLEs.

PICKING

There are five major types of ML used today. Supervised and unsupervised ML are two types that differ in the degree of human involvement at every step. Reinforcement learning is a functionally different approach to supervised and unsupervised ML. Transfer and deep learning overlap with the other types. The table below shows what might be applicable to a particular situation depending on the data at hand, required interpretability, and existing knowledge of the prediction problem.

	SUPERVISED	UNSUPERVISED	REINFORCEMENT	TRANSFER	DEEP
Learns from	inputs given outputs	inputs without outputs	objectives	inputs	other layers in the network
Needs	training and feedback data	lots of data	objectives	existing models	lots of data and computational resources

(continued)

	SUPERVISED	UNSUPERVISED	REINFORCEMENT	TRANSFER	DEEP
Good when	data is available but the algorithm is missing	it's unclear what is being looked at and/ or there are no labels	it's possible to articulate the state, action, reward, and how to modify the state based on the rewards	problems are similar, training time and computational resources are limited, and results are needed fast	there is lots of unstructured time series data (for *convolutional neural networks*) or data that's *not* independent (for *recurrent neural networks*)*
Selected methods include	random forest trees, decision trees (including random forest and gradient boosted types), regression, *support vector machines (SVMs)*, and neural networks	clustering (*k-means*, hierarchical, and others) and *Gaussian mixture models***	various, but all forms of reinforcement learning	Bayesian networks and Markov logic networks	convolutional neural networks and recurrent neural networks

*Convolutional neural networks and recurrent neural networks are explained on p. 151.

**See the glossary for definitions of these terms.

COMPOUNDING

There are many different methods for making predictions, each one generating and accumulating data in various ways. Here are some common methods, with explanations of how they generate new data as output from the model, accumulate it over time, and can be used to train models.

Diverse Disciplines

Inductive logic programming (ILP): Formal logic is a relatively straightforward form of intelligence. The programmer creates a sequence of rules that represent data, then the program generates data according to those rules. In terms of data generation, this takes place upon completing a successful experiment. As for data accumulation, no data is automatically accumulated until the programmer designs new rules or sets up a new experiment using existing rules.

Statistical analysis: There are a multitude of statistical analysis methods, such as regression analysis, that are useful for establishing rules to categorize data. In terms of data creation, the categories assigned to data points—like a demographic element—are metadata that could be useful when building another predictive model. There is no automatic data accumulation here, however, these methods can be beneficial when either running experiments to find features for ML models or just cleaning data.

Decision trees: Decision trees are structured in branches and leaves. The branches are more general observations about components in a dataset, and the leaves are the specific targets of the analysis. The way to get from the branches to the leaves is through creating and using different classes or running regressions, depending on whether the data can be classified in discrete buckets (using regression, for instance) or on a continuum from which to calculate a discrete number. With those classes and numbers, the observations (branches) grow into the predictions (leaves). In terms of data creation, the classes created in the process of building a decision tree can be valuable information, not only in running that tree but also in making other decisions in the same domain or a similar one. That is, the addition of a class or number to a piece of data is a form of metadata that could be useful when building another predictive model. As for data accumulation, decision trees can produce data at an increasing rate by adding some degree of *recursion* to the tree; that is, running over itself and voting on whether the new leaf should replace the old.

Decision networks: These are representations of finite, sequential decision-making problems in diagram form that incorporate the variables in a decision and some measure of utility for certain outcomes—that is, what would come of the decision going a certain way. Decision networks are usually structured as a directed acyclic (that is, jumping between points rather than going around in the same cyclic pattern at every run) graph. Essentially, that's a big web of possibilities to traverse in one direction. Bayesian networks are a type of decision network in which the probabilities assigned to each part of the graph are conditional on whatever happens in an earlier part of the decision cycle so that there is a probability function on each node of the graph that takes values from the nodes before it. In terms of data generation, decision networks can infer the network structure, *weights*, unobserved variables, and probability distributions from the data. This network and those distributions that are applied to each part of the network can then be used to make other decisions. When it comes to data accumulation, new weights and parameters can be inferred on each run of the network because these will change depending on the decision made on the previous run of the network.

Evolutionary algorithms: Biology inspires many types of machine learning, and evolution specifically inspires a class of systems that includes genetic algorithms. These systems figure out optimal solutions by picking the algorithms that produce the best results in each iteration, then using them in the next iteration, gradually narrowing the field of candidate algorithms. In terms of data generation, evolutionary systems generate output data with every iteration, while as for terms of data accumulation, evolutionary systems will continue to generate output data at an increasing rate until instructed to stop.

Machine Learning

Feed-forward networks: These networks run in one direction: forward. With regard to data creation, feed-forward networks create a prediction upon each run. In terms of data accumulation, feed-forward networks do not accumulate data at an increasing rate because the network does not automatically rerun itself and does not automatically add features over time.

Recurrent neural networks (RNNs): These are similar to feed-forward networks in terms of initial structure but can be applied to a sequence of inputs of indeterminate length, using the state after processing previous inputs to influence how to process the current input. In terms of data creation, recurrent neural networks create predictions at the time of output, often when the model achieves a certain degree of accuracy. In terms of data accumulation, RNNs generate predictions on every automatic run of the network, albeit at changing levels of accuracy.

Convolutional neural networks (CNNs): These are similar to deeper versions of feed-forward networks, in that there are many layers on which differential calculus is performed before generating an output. In terms of data creation, convolutional neural networks can learn features of a problem, which is valuable even if those features don't improve the accuracy of the model in which they were generated. In terms of data accumulation, convolutional neural networks accumulate these features with each automatic run of the network. The features aren't data, but they are information; use these features to figure out what to explore next and how to get more value out of incremental data by applying a different model next time.

Generative adversarial networks (GANs): GANs are networks of two (or more) ML models that are set up to challenge each other. This is like debating someone; having an intellectual sparring partner. One of the unsupervised models (the generator, typically a deconvolutional neural network) generates new models from what it can infer about the relevant data, while the other model (the discriminator, typically a convolutional neural network) evaluates the candidate models against the true data distribution. The generator is trying to come up with candidates that the discriminator thinks are close to the true data distribution but, in fact, will eventually generate something novel—outside the data distribution—as a sort of test. This is somewhat counterintuitive but important with respect to data generation. In terms of data creation, GANs come up with features that the designer of the model didn't even consider because the evaluation of the model feeds back into the next run such that both the generator and discriminator create new data distributions in the next run. In terms of data accumulation, GANs can accumulate data at an increasing rate because the new models may be much more effective than the previous models. With each automatic run of the network, GANs add features until there is no more discrimination to do.

Reinforcement learning (RL): Reinforcement learning, an area of ML, involves developing agents that optimize for a reward—in other words, creating a (software) agent that has ML at its disposal to reach a goal, such as winning a computer game. In terms of data creation, the agent collects observations each time it performs an action, and those observations may be novel because the creator never programmed a model to take the actions the RL agent took. These agents accumulate data constantly: observing the state of the system, acting to change it, observing the effect of their actions, and so on.

THE DATA CREATED AND ACCUMULATED BY ML METHODS

METHOD	DATA CREATED	DATA ACCUMULATED
Inductive logic programming	Rules	None
Statistical analysis	Categories	None
Decision trees	Classes	Performance of classes
Decision networks	Inferred network structure, weights, unobserved variables, and probability distributions	Weights and parameters
Evolutionary algorithms	Algorithm performance	Algorithm performance
Feed-forward networks	Predictions	None
Recurrent neural networks	Predictions	Predictions
Convolutional neural networks	Features	Features
Generative adversarial networks	Features	Features
Reinforcement learning	Observational	Observational

CONCLUSION

Getting started with machine learning is easier than ever, even as the frontier of cutting-edge research is shifting faster than ever. Picking up a basic framework and running data through it is as good a starting point as any. I see companies do this every day, only later digging into the harder problems of customizing the components of these models as necessary to solve a customer's problem.

Picking the right method for the job depends both on what you've got to work with and what you're trying to predict. Once you have some ML models working, it may be time to take a step back and consider how they may contribute to a core company asset. The power of AI is in the information built up over time, and lots of that information is in the data itself—*what* it learns. However, AI also generates data about *how* it learns in the rules, features, predictions, classes, structures, parameters, and other things output upon every turn of the crank.

PLAYBOOK

- **Pick a machine learning method based on available data.** Supervised learning needs training and feedback data, whereas unsupervised ML just requires lots of data.

- **Some models need an objective.** Reinforcement-learned models need objectives. Other forms of ML generally do not, and they will even surface information without objectives.

- **Learn to learn.** Some AIs generate data about how they learn, accumulating a valuable asset to leverage when searching for solutions to new problems.

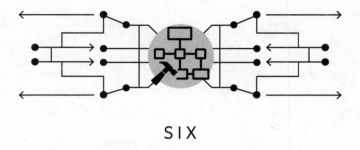

SIX

MANAGING THE MODELS

The next challenge is taking artificial intelligence from the lab to the real world. AI-First products are sticky but need contact points with existing software, processes, and systems, so we start this chapter with best practices for customer implementations.

We see media reports of AIs "going crazy": generating biased or offensive output and making questionable decisions. The ongoing challenge is to make sure that the models don't break or lose touch with reality. AI-First products are powerful because they constantly adapt, evolve, and spawn new data, but this constant change makes them hard to manage, like a multidimensional balancing act of the following factors.

Experimentation vs. Implementation

Freedom to experiment leads to powerful models, but those models need to be implemented in the real world in order to generate value.

Decentralization vs. Centralization

The expertise that informs a model's features is decentralized—spread across and between organizations—but the software infrastructure on which the models run is centralized.

Testing and Observing

We can expose mechanical problems in a test environment but have to put the models into the real world to make observations from which to learn.

The ideal model management system allows AI-First companies to run decentralized experiments, rigorously test models, and monitor them once they start learning from real data. Crucially, the ideal model management system lets the models learn without breaking.

Creating a closed-loop system that validates the output of a model before running it again keeps the models in check. The big idea proposed in this section is the ML management loop: an automated system to continuously train, version, deploy, test, monitor, and fix models. You don't need to get this whole loop running in order to get started; you can be successful with just part of it in motion. This chapter aims to increase your awareness of what could go wrong, and when, so that you can stay one step ahead of potential problems. Here we'll relate model management to concepts familiar to those in the technology industry such as agile development, DevOps, and *statistical process control (SPC)*, while also introducing novel ideas specific to managing intelligent systems. We have two diagrams to guide you through the two parts to this chapter: Implementation and Management.

STEPS TO ACCEPTANCE

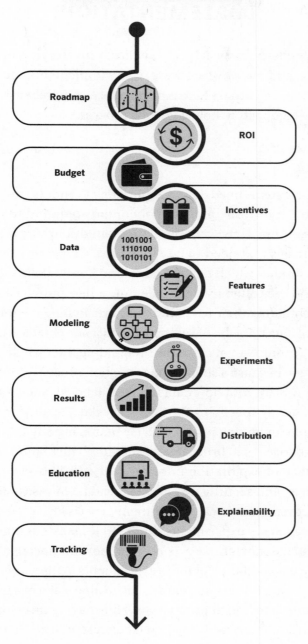

Roadmap

ROI

Budget

Incentives

Data

Features

Modeling

Experiments

Results

Distribution

Education

Explainability

Tracking

IMPLEMENTATION

Taking a model from the lab to live typically involves lots of people, processes, and pieces of software. Every implementation is idiosyncratic, so the purpose here is not to offer a comprehensive guide but rather signposts to help guide the process.

Data

Intelligent systems need data. A multitude of vendors can manage the extract, transform, and load operations required to get data from customers. However, there are often duplicates and other idiosyncrasies that need to be reconciled. Customers may have opinions around which tables to keep and how to define data elements, and they often use implementing a new product as a catalyst for rebuilding their data infrastructure. Pulling the minimum amount of data from the fewest tables in just one database can help to avoid the problem of customers rebuilding their whole data infrastructure, because a single data extraction process is unlikely to reveal a problem with how data is stored, labeled, and so forth. In any case, tightly specifying the necessary data, leading the teams responsible for getting it, and actively managing any ETL vendor selection process can bring about faster implementation.

The stage of exploration informs trade-offs between cost, latency, scale, and security when choosing data infrastructure. For example, to run small-scale experiments, cost is less important because small-scale experiments don't need many computational resources. Latency, though, is more important because quickly obtaining results allows for more experiments in the same amount of time. Scaling is less important at the testing stage but more important after moving to production. Thus paying more on a per-row basis for a highly available (low-latency) database to store data for experiments makes sense at the experimentation phase but not at the production phase. You might select a cloud vendor for your production database that can quickly and automatically spin up new servers for customers all around the world. Picking the right database and data infrastructure for an AI-First company is more complicated than for a traditional software company because AI-First products have regular training, test, and production cycles— each with different cost, latency, scale, and security needs.

Software

Intelligent systems sometimes have an application with a user interface to deliver the predictions, but other times they directly integrate with existing systems. For example, an AI-First CRM company might build a new application for salespeople to use every day, or it might feed recommendations into an existing CRM, such as Salesforce. In the latter case, where the system feeds into another front-end application, it will need to hook into that application through an API. That's easier when the application has an open API (Salesforce again), and more difficult when it's a closed (and often paid) API, like SAP, or when it has no API at all, requiring a custom integration. Building an application is a totally new software project with a different set of considerations that are beyond the scope of this book.

Security

Intelligent systems often use high volumes of data. With more data comes more risk, especially if that data includes sensitive information such as a person's physical location or financial information. Each dataset may have different users, permissions, and external access requirements. For example, customers may access the experimentation dataset to see results but not the test set in case they interrupt a test. Experimental data might be completely synthetic in cases where the customer's data is subject to strict privacy regulations, as with healthcare data. Production data may be completely obfuscated when it needs to be contained to the customer's environment, requiring self-contained models that can run on the customer's premises or a system that, for example, utilizes privacy-preserving encryption. Managing access is often a spectral consideration mapping to the existing permissions of internal and external stakeholders.

Some perceptive, intelligent systems require high volumes of data from sensors such as cameras, and each of those sensors is a potential vector of attack for hackers. Accessing databases through a connected camera, doorbell, or toothbrush is something hackers can and will do. Modeling the software running on those sensors, understanding security flaws, and keeping every sensor up-to-date is imperative for AI-First companies.

Sensors

AI-First companies building intelligent systems that obtain data from sensors may need a separate engineering and field operations team to manage them. Shipping sensors from manufacturers to customers is a logistics challenge, while installing sensors involves creating fixtures, routing power, and connecting them to the Internet. Maintaining sensors presents environmental challenges, such as making a thermal sensor work in a cold environment or preventing theft. There are a multitude of implementation difficulties in managing fleets of sensors, each specific to the type of sensor and its environment. Budgeting for these implementation costs—separate from the hardware expenses—is crucial when pricing deals.

Services

Implementing software often involves highly specialized services. Third-party vendors, commonly known as *systems integrators (SIs)* and *independent software vendors (ISVs),* perform these services and may be worth involving in implementations where doing the work in-house is neither economical nor strategic. AI-First companies may especially benefit from working with SIs where the work of integrating the software is separable from the work of integrating customer data and training models. For example, when predicting where to place a delivery truck so that it's ready for the next shipment, data may be in a legacy *enterprise resource planning (ERP)* product such as SAP. Therefore, it may be best to work with an SAP-specific SI to acquire that data rather than learn how to do it by working through the tomes of SAP documentation.

SIs can be particularly helpful when implementation calls for installing and maintaining hardware. There are hardware-specific SIs that partner with manufacturers to install and maintain their sensors. They know how to wire them together, connect them to the Internet, and pipe data into the database. Their experience and professional relationships often allow for a more seamless installation process, faster resolution times, and more available inventory for customers as they scale up.

Staffing

The implementation team for an AI-First product may include a data validator (to check if the data is high quality) or data engineer (to clean the data), data scientists (to run the experiments), and ML engineers (to turn them into models). This is in addition to standard software implementation roles such as product manager, application developer, developer operations engineer, and legal.

Communicating results to customers may require hiring a separate team. Those who are skilled at interpreting model outputs and presenting them to customers can help build customer enthusiasm during the pilot phase and ensure adoption in the production phase. These people typically have a background in consulting or another professional service, with a good facility for data science. Hiring a team to create and give these presentations to customers on a regular basis can lead to higher, eventual acceptance of an AI-First product.

Acceptance

Acceptance of AI-First products can be challenging for both technical and political reasons. The degree of integration with existing systems can be deep and the degree of change to decision-making processes can be significant. Here are some practices that may improve the chances that an AI-First product is accepted by customers, mapped to a timeline and explained below.

Technical

- **MAKE SURE IT WORKS.** Expectations will collide with reality at some point, and acceptance or rejection will be final. Meeting customers' expectations of AI-First products is hard because the product's promise is a prediction about something that will happen in the real world. Compare this to software products, that merely deliver the features in the specification. The first step is to investigate the data available to the model. Is there a tractable AI-based solution to the customer's problem?

- **DON'T GET DISTRACTED BY DATA CLEANING.** Organizing data so that it's in one place, clean, completely labeled, and stored cost-effectively is a sizeable, perpetual hurdle. Customers will be at different stages on their journeys to organizing data, and adopting an AI-First product may be a catalyst for a data organization project. This might be in everyone's long-term interest because organized data allows for faster, better, and cheaper experimentation with AI—among many other benefits—but balancing this long-term interest with the short-term challenge of acceptance is the immediate concern. Get the AI-First product in the hands of customers without embarking on a yearlong data-lake project by manually pulling only the necessary data. This may be somewhat costly on a per-project basis but better than never finishing the project at all.

■ **SET A REALISTIC SCHEDULE.** Customers are constantly juggling projects and need to organize their time efficiently. Providing them with a realistic road map allows them to prioritize the time it will take to implement the product. Without such a road map, there's a risk that one proof of concept will lead into another unplanned POC to prove something that wasn't anticipated, reducing enthusiasm for the product. The purchase order or request for another POC may be denied. Creating this road map and distributing it to all stakeholders sets realistic expectations for the implementation.

■ **REGULARLY RETRAIN.** Retraining the model on new data and then deploying the retrained models quickly can develop a positive feedback loop of customers seeing that the model responds to the data they input, encouraging them to input more data.

■ **DEVELOP FEATURES FAST.** Just as in software development, iterating quickly on customer feedback generates more feedback and builds confidence along the way.

Political—Procurement Stage

■ **AUGMENT, DON'T AUTOMATE.** Be sure to position the product as something that augments human experts, to fend off the fear of replacement by AI.

- **VALUE REVENUE OVER COSTS.** Customers will appreciate the ways in which an AI-First product may save them money. However, making money is more exciting than saving it. Think about ways in which the AI-First product may earn revenue from new opportunities to build excitement around the product and improve both parts of the ROI equation.

- **CREATE UNIT-LEVEL ROI.** Create a ROI calculus with customers for each of their business units. Ultimately, deliver returns on the customer's investment at a company level.

- **SECURE SUFFICIENT BUDGET.** Make sure customers have a budget that covers all the ancillary costs of implementation, from data labeling to buying sensors. For example, a large bill for cameras that customers can't afford might mean never getting the data needed to train an image recognition model.

- **SET INCENTIVES.** Work with customers to set incentives for key stakeholders to make the implementation successful. These incentives can be on the customer side—for example, a cash bonus for completing an implementation milestone—or they may be linked to a shared milestone, such as reaching a certain level of accuracy.

- **PRACTICE ACCOUNTABILITY.** Work with customers to help ensure that the people most central to the implementation process—data engineers and integration engineers come to mind—are accountable for completing their tasks.

Political—POC Stage

- **REDUCE THE TIME TO VALUE.** Show results as quickly as possible. This can fend off skepticism about whether the system will actually work, or that it's just theoretical research without a practical effect, or that the project will drag on and on, or that integration is impossible.

- **BUILD FOR THE AUDIENCE.** The person making the purchase decision isn't always the same person using the product. Building product enhancements such as reporting or administrative dashboards for the purchaser can help to close the sale.

- **ENGAGE WITH EXPERIMENTS.** Regularly updating key customer stakeholders can improve the rate of acceptance by building both trust and understanding around the product. Hosting regular sessions to explain hypotheses and presenting experimental results can encourage high customer engagement. These sessions may help customers develop an appreciation of the progression to predictive perfection with probabilistic systems and offer feedback on hypotheses.

Political—Execution Stage

- **GAIN EARLY AND BROAD DISTRIBUTION.** Acceptance of AI-First products can be a self-fulfilling prophecy: getting more people to use the product leads to more feedback data, improving the product and convincing more people to use it. AI-First products are thus best when distributed vertically, up and down the management chain, **and** horizontally, in each business unit, as quickly as possible. The alternative—giving it to a single analytics team that works horizontally across business units—can lead to a lack of acceptance because the horizontal team doesn't have the power to get adoption, or the ability to effectively transfer knowledge through training, or the motivation to complete implementations in every business unit. Working with customers to vertically distribute the product into every business unit may require collaborating with them on a new organizational structure or attracting a high-level executive to advocate for the product's adoption across the organization.

- **PROVIDE EXECUTIVE EDUCATION.** Management is direction, and good direction requires detailed knowledge of the tasks at hand. Educating customers' executive and management teams on the technology behind an AI-First product to the point of becoming fluent in terminology and gaining a fundamental understanding of the models' functions will ensure that they are equipped to offer specific directions to their organization's implementation teams. Provide materials for the customer to present education sessions or engage outside educational institutions or consulting firms to run them.

- **EMBED EXPLAINABILITY.** Features that allow customers to understand why the AI made a given prediction not only foster trust but also give them ideas for how to improve the underlying model where it gave an incorrect prediction.

- **SET UP USAGE TRACKING.** Usage tracking ensures that customers are engaging with the product. This is something common with software products, but it is often overlooked when the usage modality of the product isn't as simple as clicking buttons on a website. AI-First products may necessitate novel ways to track usage through API calls, reads of a database, tagging, or other approaches.

These practices address the technical and social dimensions of acceptance before, during, and after a model goes into production. Considering which to pursue, and at which point in time, depends on the degree of acceptance needed at each stage.

THE MACHINE LEARNING MANAGEMENT LOOP

Customers want models that are accurate and don't break. This means that the models need to learn from real-world data quickly and reliably. Manual monitoring systems work only so fast, so we need a continuous, automatic model management system like the one proposed in this chapter: to take output from running the model—both observations and errors—and then figure out what's needed to keep the model running, improve accuracy, and reduce errors.

THE MACHINE LEARNING MANAGEMENT LOOP

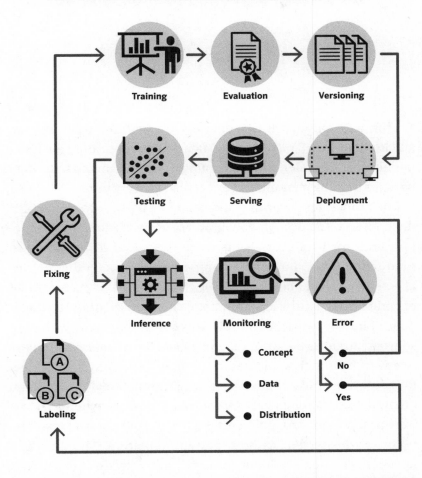

This system allows for continuous incorporation of real-world data. Let's walk through the parts of this system: training, versioning, deployment, serving, testing, and monitoring. Chapter 7, "Measuring the Loop," covers the evaluation step.

Training

This is the step before evaluation and deployment, when models are often re-created. The point to make about monitoring during the training step is to separate datasets.

Training   Evaluation

This is the point at which datasets are split into training, test, and holdout sets. Separating test data avoids confirming the functionality of the model, whereas testing the model on the same data used for training guarantees perfect results every time.

The model starts learning and changing when it goes into production, so set aside a holdout group of users, customers, production lines, or whatever else is to be measured *before* going to production. This allows later comparisons between the metrics affected by AI and not affected by AI. It is a completely separate set of entities that use the legacy system, and is quarantined so that it doesn't interact with the AI at all. This can be easy to do with pure software products but more difficult where the AI interacts with the real world through an actuator, robot, or other physical device. Pure software products often have flagging functionality in order to offer different features to different user segments, whereas hardware products may require setting up a separate physical manifestation of the system without certain actuators. The ancillary benefit of creating a holdout group is that it provides a good basis of comparison for customers as they make a decision about whether to invest in the AI.

Incidentally, showing customers the output at each training step can yield a reaction about the validity of that output. They can not only tell if the model's prediction output makes sense but also perhaps offer ideas for more predictive features to include based on their experience. For example, they've seen that every time it rains, drivers prefer to wait longer at each stop on a route, extending delivery times. This may cause you to incorporate weather data into your model and train on that data to see if the correlation observed by your customer is statistically true. If so, you can use weather as a predictive feature of delivery times. Sharing the results of models in the training phase is analogous to mocking up interfaces for customers as you develop software applications.

Versioning

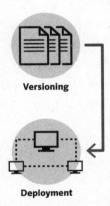

Versioning

Deployment

Keeping versions of models provides a basis for making improvements and allows reversion to old models if the new one isn't as good. The challenge with *versioning* model code is that it needs to be versioned in tandem with the training data because the interaction of the model with data generates the output. *Data* refers to both the values and the *schema* (the form common to all values) in which those values are stored, with code calling objects in the database according to the schema. We also have the code for the software that displays the output and runs the computing infrastructure. So, we have model code, data values, data schema, and software code. Versioning in all four dimensions leads to many permutations. Keeping one dimension relatively constant makes going back through the versions much easier.

Versioning models is relatively straightforward because there are established ways to version computer code. Versioning data, however, is less straightforward, given that some models train on very large datasets. We can't use code-versioning tools to track versions of the dataset because they do not scale to handle large, unordered datasets. Nor can we store every dataset at every point in time because that is very costly. We don't consider versioning the schema, assuming instead that we can infer the schema from the values. Data infrastructure with features such as metadata management, similarity modeling, and automated data catalogue creation makes this inference process more reliable. Versioning data is hard, so we prefer to version the code behind the models as a first step, and consider data versioning after properly versioning models and adding metadata to the database. Data versioning tools compress and mark the datasets at a point in time and then store them.

Reproducibility

One goal of this process is reproducibility. Tracking changes to code and models, data packages, tools, and other dependencies allows others to reproduce work. Reproducibility is important for both the training and evaluation steps, but it can be challenging, particularly for the training step and, indeed, intractable when using deep learning. This is important in many contexts, from academia to regulated industries, where customers may have to reproduce and explain a model's output later.

Deployment

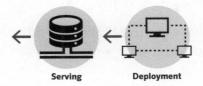

Serving   Deployment

There are a multitude of ways to deploy and serve predictions to customers, starting with a printed report, to augmenting their minds and bodies as they make their decisions. Go the way of your customer, meeting them where they are.

1. **Reports:** Print the prediction and perhaps an explanation in a report.

2. **Spreadsheets:** Provide the prediction and some ways to manipulate the key variables or change the underlying data in a spreadsheet. This may work only for simple models made up of functions available in programs such as Excel.

3. **Dashboards:** Provide the prediction in a Web-based, automatically updated dashboard.

4. **Templates:** Provide the prediction in a Web-based, automatically updated dashboard and allow customers to manipulate the key variables or upload new data using a form.

5. **Integrations:** Provide the prediction to another application, such as a CRM or ERP, and set up a two-way data pipeline between the model and that application to ensure that the predictions stay up-to-date.

6. **Applications:** Provide the prediction in an application and allow customers to manipulate the key variables or upload new data using buttons in the application.

7. **Application programming interfaces:** Provide access to the prediction through an API and allow customers to provide feedback data or upload new data through the API.

8. **Augmentations:** Provide the prediction in context, through hardware such as a wearable computer that delivers predictions in the user's field of vision through eyeglasses, on a watch, or projected onto a nearby surface.

Testing

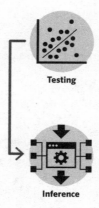

Testing

Inference

Testing models is less deterministic than testing software. Validating models is for figuring out if the model's output makes sense in a physical environment, whereas the purpose of validating code is to make sure it will run in a virtual (computing) environment. Testing models involves checking the assumptions, sensitivities, and sampling of data to confirm that they line up with the real world.

Automated and manual tests achieve the above. Automated, rule-based tests take the form of scripts run against the model's output: for example, cats are never purple, and Coke bottles are never yellow. Automated, control-group tests take the form of checking the model's output with a dataset that represents the "ground truth" and seeing how much the model's predictions deviate from it. Manual, human-operated tests take the form of checking the output against manually sampled data, personal observations, and common sense. The output is correct if it makes sense to the analyst. Increasing automated test coverage and reducing manual work over time is ideal, but it depends on the degree to which the models in use are explainable or decomposable into parts with relatively simple mechanics and thus easier to understand, and the dynamism of the operating environment.

The first step in most testing processes often entails checking the output to see if it makes statistical sense. Manufacturers use statistical process control to manage product quality. SPC can help in managing data quality by spotting anomalous results in model output and then tracking them back to changes in the underlying distribution of data, although this is very difficult when using deep learning, for example. Where the distribution of data on which the model trained differs from the distribution observed in the real world, go back and access better data, retrain the model, and redeploy it into the real world.

The middle steps in a testing process are idiosyncratic to the modeling task. Depending on the PUT, try changing the parameters, *hyperparameters*, features, capacity (data), and number of training *epochs* (set time periods for training) of the model. Setting up a table of correlations between features and labels, also known as a *confusion matrix*, can be helpful at this point. Think of this as a "heat map" that helps one focus on the areas where the model needs to improve: the lightly shaded boxes. Look down at the x axis to get the label, then retrieve the examples generated by the model with that label (the predicted label) to understand why they might be generating weak correlations with reality (the true label). Iterate over the same metrics, trying to improve performance. Ideally there would be a line of 100% correlations going from the top left to the bottom right.

CONFUSION MATRIX

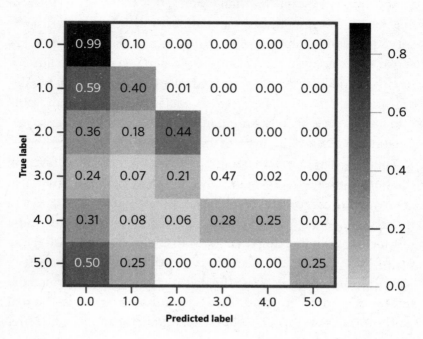

The final step in most testing processes is *integration testing*: making sure the model code executes properly in the customer's computing environment, as well as on the chosen infrastructure and as part of the process to deploy all software code, not just model code. This important step is not covered here because there are existing tools and best practices to test software code.

Monitoring

Model performance issues have many causes, from training volumes growing too large for databases, to models becoming too big for available computer memory, to poor validation of inputs, to the law of large numbers affecting excessive variance across a high vol-

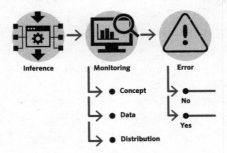

ume of predictions. Production monitoring ensures both quality and reliability of the models. *Quality* pertains to performance; *reliability*, to accuracy and stability. Within quality, performance issues relate to deployment: the quality of the code and infrastructure. Many of the best practices come from software engineering and are beyond the scope of this book. Let's focus on reliability for deployment: accuracy and stability.

Accuracy

Statistical, quantitative measures such as accuracy, relevance, and loss are useful to monitor models in production. Semantic, qualitative measures, including whether a customer accepts a model's output or contributes verbal feedback, are also useful. The combination of both indicates whether the model delivers the requisite predictive quality. Both statistical and semantic measures of model quality come together in the concepts of model drift and bias.

Stability

Drift is when something diverges from reality. There are a few ways a model can diverge from reality:

1. *Concept drift* is when the idea behind the prediction changes based on real-world observations. For instance, let's say that

you thought you needed to predict whether a driver would arrive before five o'clock in the afternoon, so that customers received their orders, but you actually needed to predict the likelihood of theft from the customer's front porch.

2. *Data drift* refers to the distribution underlying the prediction changing to such an extent that it no longer represents the real world. Here is an example: you thought that customers buy batteries throughout the year, but it turns out that they tend to buy batteries after an extreme weather event. Data drift also occurs when data is no longer available or properly formed, as when you lose a source of location data because a developer cuts you off from its API.

The method to address drift depends on the type of drift. Concept drift requires redoing the features of the model, then retraining, while data drift requires tracking down new data and then retraining. Redoing models, gathering new data, and retraining can all be expensive, and careful measurement of drift allows for wise decisions about whether to incur these costs.

Detecting drift using model performance, data quality, and product efficacy metrics can reveal the source of low reliability. Model performance metrics that we explicate in Chapter 7, "Measuring the Loop," include those around predictive accuracy, such as an *F1 score*. Data-quality metrics include those around label coverage. Product efficacy metrics get to the true customer ROI, such as failure rates on a production line. The interaction between these metrics is also important: if the distribution of data changes but the predictions are still accurate, that just means the world changed.

One approach to ensuring the accuracy of benchmarks for these metrics is similar to that taken during the model training phase: keep a control group, which delivers ground truth data about model performance.

Measuring model drift on a regular basis is imperative, given that the world changes gradually, suddenly, and regularly. We can measure gradual changes only if we receive metrics over time; sudden changes, only if we get metrics close to real time; and regular changes, only if we accumulate metrics at the same interval—for example, every season.

Bias

The issue of *bias* in ML is both ethical and technical. We deal with the technical here and summarize management of machine bias by saying it's the same way we often manage human bias: with hard constraints. Setting constraints on what the model can predict, who accesses those predictions, limits on feedback data, acceptable uses of the predictions, and more requires effort when designing the system but ensures appropriate alerting. Additionally, setting standards for training data can increase the likelihood that it considers a wide range of inputs. Speaking to the designer of the model is the best way to reach an understanding of the risks of bias inherent in their approach. Consider automatic actions such as shutdown or alerting after setting these constraints.

Data Quality

Data-quality processes ensure that models get the data they need. The data pipeline may have lots of parts, and each of those may break, causing the model or something that sits on top of the model, such as a dashboard, to break. There are data-quality-focused products, and some data vendors may provide data-quality metrics. Here are some examples of what a data-quality product can monitor:

- **Missing sources.** Third-party and internal data sources sometimes fail, cut off, or shut down.

- **Missing values.** Functions in models have certain variables and get values to populate those variables from databases. When the database changes but the functions calling the values from that database do not change, the functions won't be able to find the values, and the model will break. For example, the functions will be looking for a table name that doesn't exist or a deleted value.

- **Incomplete data.** Sometimes a function calls for a lot of data but doesn't need all of it to execute. When it doesn't get all of the data it needs, it may still execute but generate poor predictions. Knowing what data is missing may help to figure out the source of inaccurate predictions. This is different from where the value is required and missing, in which case the function will not execute at all.

- **Missing labels.** Human labelers may fail to properly label a data point that's required by the model. The data may be labeled, just not in a particularly descriptive way: for example, labeling someone walking across a street as "person" rather than "person jumping in front of a car." The model may still be able to learn from improper labels, but it may cause problems over time. Data-quality processes can run checks on the label to make sure it's useful to the model. This is a variation of incomplete data.

- **Data distribution drift.** This is the more nuanced and advanced part of data-quality monitoring. Data-quality processes and products measure drift by monitoring the data distribution with statistical process controls and other methods.

- **Perturbation.** Preempt data-quality issues by deliberately modifying data to see if it causes problems further down in the data pipeline.

Rework

The final step in the ML management loop is making adjustments based on monitoring output.

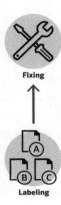

Adjustments will be necessary at some point because the world is always changing. This may be less true in more deterministic systems such as a robotized factory line, but tolerances are never zero—change is a given. Therefore, it's worth knowing the ways to adjust models, from doing nothing to rebuilding the whole system.

1. **DO NOTHING.** The model stays the same and, indeed, should stay the same because the goal is for it to bring systems back to a deterministic state, like a rules-based system—for instance, always filtering emails with highly offensive content as spam even if marked as "Not spam" by users.

2. **ASK QUESTIONS.** Asking customers for their interpretations of what has changed in either the accuracy, data, or efficacy may yield valuable ideas for adjustments.

3. **ADD DATA.** Get more data to understand an edge case directly from customers and labelers or through synthetic generation. Incorporating synthetic data generation into the

model management loop could even automate the process of fixing models where they drift or break due to a lack of data.

4. **RETRAIN.** When the underlying reality is seasonal or suspected to be out of date, and the cost of training is sufficiently low, periodically retrain the model on new data.

5. **REFIT.** If the underlying distribution is changing but not because reality is changing, data collection is perhaps causing a problem that needs correction such that the data is more like a normal distribution or representative of reality. An example would be if you initially notice that people enter a store only when it's really hot outside, only to realize later that the sensor measuring the number of people entering the store used to collect the data doesn't work when it's cold.

6. **REWEIGHT.** When the underlying distribution changes less frequently than is suspected necessary to represent reality, change the model to favor more recent data. This is different from periodic refitting because it's not refitting the data to a different distribution, just changing the weights. Set time windows around the data—for example, what is considered to be a "season" in the industry in question—so that the model trains only on data from a specific time period.

7. **REDO.** This can mean changing the predictive features of the model or adding features. This takes us back to questions about what to predict, running data science experiments to figure out which features to develop, back testing the new models, and deciding whether to implement them.

Choose to automate the manual processes above later if you're doing them manually at every run of the loop. Model management and AutoML systems will often automate adjustment through continuous retraining.

Redeploy

Redeploying the retrained, refitted, reweighted, or redone model is the final step in the loop. Redeploy the model to some or all customers, add short-term tests to make sure the new model doesn't break right away, and then test it at regular intervals. Figuring out how and when to redeploy models is important because it can be costly and affects how to measure the system going forward.

Rethink

Taking a step back after running the loop, or a few loops, allows for developing better ways to measure the system, and saves time and money in the future.

The first thing to measure—or just log—is what changed in the model, when, and why. The next is to reconsider the dataset used to validate the model. This probably will not change unless there's a wholesale change to the model, because the original purpose of the validation set was to provide a benchmark for the model. The third thing to consider is whether to change any of the core metrics that cover model performance, concept drift, and data drift. Finally, ask the customer if the new model changes the way they think about ROI.

Changing the data pipeline may avoid similar types and degrees of model, concept, and data drift in the future. Systematically collecting new data through a labeling operation or getting feedback data can be a way to keep models working when data pipelines break. Where the drift occurred due to shoddy data quality, implement better data governance policies. Finally, consider updating data by refreshing some or all of the pipeline more often.

CHECKLIST

Here's a checklist that captures everything monitored in this system, in addition to measurements of their quality (performance) and reliability (accuracy).

❏ *Models*

☐ *Quality metrics*
☐ Accuracy
☐ Relevance
☐ Reliability
☐ Performance

☐ *Holdout*
☐ Compare to the old holdout set
☐ Create a new holdout set for this model

☐ *ROI*
☐ Quantitative ROI calculus for the customer
☐ Other feedback on the new model for the customer

❏ *Data*

☐ *Reliability metrics*
☐ Model
☐ Concept
☐ Data

☐ *Governance changes*
☐ Increase labeling compliance
☐ Improve metadata management
☐ Enforce standards

☐ *Pipeline changes*
☐ Remove failure points
☐ Modify poor data sources
☐ Add quality data sources

CONCLUSION

Getting machine learning models to work reliably, every day, is quite hard. There are still a lot of tools required to manage these models as well as we manage software today that haven't been built. Most of the companies I see build their own processes and tools, but my hope is that in the next few years, the ecosystem will develop to make this part of building an AI-First company much easier. Maybe you even have an idea for a product after considering the ideal loop presented in this chapter.

Successful implementation of AI-First products involves many novel considerations but you don't have to work through them all at once; you can be successful by starting with just part of the system suggested in this chapter. Managing AI-First products postimplementation involves developing an automated system for training, versioning, deploying, testing, and monitoring. The lessons from running this system make the model better over time. There is a lot to consider, however: keep in mind that what we're ultimately building is a learning effect, so that we can learn bit by bit, incorporating our lessons in a multitude of ways. You don't have to get everything perfect like you do when launching a software product; you just have to manage customers' expectations and, hopefully, improve the predictions.

PLAYBOOK

- **Keep models close to reality.** Intelligent systems are powerful because they constantly adapt, evolve, and spawn new data, but be aware that they can run away from reality. Constantly getting feedback keeps models in check.

- **Strike a balance.** The ideal model management system allows for decentralized experiments, rigorous testing of models, and monitoring in real-world data.

- **Don't drown in a data lake.** Tightly specify the necessary data, lead the teams responsible for accessing it, and actively manage data-related vendor selection to quickly implement AI-First products.

- **Set security parameters for every dataset.** Experimentation, testing, and production require different levels of security. Customers in regulated industries may need to run models on their premises without ever touching their data.

- **Outsource implementations that involve sensors.** Implementing and managing sensors involve significant logistics, industrial design, IT, and environmental challenges. Outsource this to a systems integrator that works with the sensor manufacturer.

- **Communication ensures a smooth implementation.** Data validators and engineers clear up inconsistencies in customers' data. Data translators communicate early results. Both can ensure a smooth implementation and ultimate acceptance of AI-First products.

- **Involve customers in training models.** Demonstrating the output at each training step can yield commonsense feedback and ideas for new features.

- **Customers want models that are accurate in the real world, not just in the lab.** Quickly incorporate real-world data and make models automatically learn from that data.

- **Acceptance of AI is a surmountable challenge.** Get early and broad distribution, make sure the AI works, lower time to value, create a realistic road map, promote engagement with experiments, provide executive education, retrain regularly, build features fast, augment (don't automate), embed explainability, incentivize the right people, ensure accountability, add buffers to budgets, measure usage, set business unit-level ROI, and focus on delivering revenue (not reducing costs).

- **Model management is not code management.** Model management needs to manage both data and code, rather than just code.

- **Version code and manage metadata before trying to version data.** Versioning data is hard and expensive. Focus on versioning model code first.

- **The goal of versioning is reproducibility.** Reproducibility is particularly important in academia and regulated industries. Add software packages, coding tools, and other dependencies that may enhance someone else's ability to replicate results to versioning systems.

- **Split up training, test, and production data.** Testing on training data always gets a perfect score. Keeping a holdout set keeps models honest.

- **Deploy predictions in the form that customers prefer.** That could be in a report, spreadsheet, dashboard, or template, integrated into another software product, as a stand-alone application, through an API, or in a piece of hardware.

(continued)

- **Test.** Use statistical measures for data quality, accuracy measures for model quality, and a correlation matrix for relevance. Don't forget to check that the code runs alongside existing software.

- **Keep an eye on drift.** Whether it's the concept or data, don't let predictions get too removed from reality.

- **Deal with bias by setting hard constraints.** Restrict what the model can output, control access, limit feedback data, and make acceptable uses of the predictions clear to all stakeholders.

- **Give models the data they need.** Constantly monitor data for missing sources, values, and labels. Proactively perturb data to catch quality issues before they break something.

- **The world is always changing, so models will too.** Retrain, refit, reweight, redo, and redeploy. Automate later.

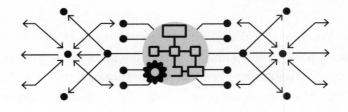

SEVEN

MEASURING THE LOOP

We start the chapter by defining loops, thinking about the nature of their motion and comparing them to the well-worn concept of a *moat*. We then provide some ways to pick the right problems to solve with AI based on the payoff of solving particular problems, data required to get the AI working, and potential for the AI to drift. These conceptual parts of the chapter are followed by two technical sections, one providing a primer on common methods used to measure the accuracy of machine learning models and the second providing a way to account for the various costs of building an AI-First company.

The big idea in this chapter is that DLEs have a dynamic, looping motion that's different from a moat. Conceiving of them as a loop provides a basis for picking the proper products to build, measuring competitive advantage, assessing risks, and making money. This is a guide to lighting up loops and understanding when they lapse.

We start the chapter by defining loops, thinking about the nature of their motion and comparing them to the well-worn concept of a "moat." We then provide some ways to pick the right (and wrong) problems to solve with AI based on the payoff of solving particular problems, data required to get the AI working, and potential for the AI to drift. These two conceptual parts of the chapter are followed by two more technical sections, one that provides a primer on common methods used to measure the accuracy of machine learning models and the second providing a way to account for the various costs of building an AI-First company.

LOOPS

This book first defined DLEs. Now we add dynamism to that definition to describe the motion of DLEs: *looping.*

Remember that there are three parts to a DLE.

1. *Inputs:* access to unique data.

2. *Process:* capabilities to process data.

3. *Networks:* models to learn over the processed data.

The first two parts can have their own internal loops, as in the example of a robot scouring the world to collect data or a machine learning technique to process data. However, the higher-level loop of a DLE gets started only after the first two parts are done and the models create a data network effect, thereby completing the process of building a DLE.

These loops are self-reinforcing and powerful because they generate their own data, endogenously and continuously, serving up predictions and collecting new data from observations. This is the power of data network effects and thus DLEs: they are self-sustaining and grow very fast.

Inherent in the motion of a loop is repeatability; loops go round and round. Competitive advantage can't compound if it doesn't

LOOPS ON LOOPS

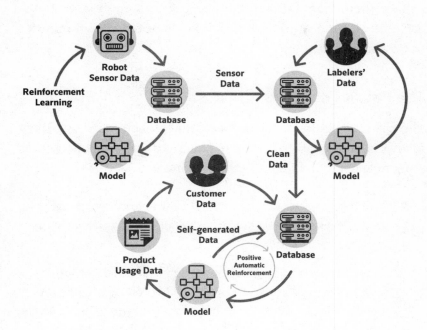

repeat. Data learning loops go round with each batch of feedback data. Every run of the loop generates a prediction that customers take into the real world, having an effect on the real world, that the model observes. The model then does some learning, generates a new prediction, and so on.

For example, an AI-First product generates a prediction that there won't be any pasta on the shelf of the supermarket in fifteen minutes, so it alerts the stocker, who goes and checks the shelf after lunch. What he sees confirms the prediction: no more pasta. So, he makes a note in his app and restocks the shelf. Meanwhile, the video camera aimed at the shelf saw that there was pasta, then no pasta, and, finally, pasta again. The AI receives that information from the camera and from the stocker's notes in the app, learning that the prediction was on target and that the pasta was restocked because the stocker did his job. This confirms that the last run of the loop was a good one, which increases the confidence around its next prediction, putting it in front of the stocker a few hours earlier next time, so that the shelf is restocked within minutes rather than hours.

The Physics of Loops

There is a fascinating set of physical principles behind loops. What follows is a rather abstract view of loops as a sort of engine: first as a steam engine* and then as a data engine.

1. Two things must react against each other to generate something. Think about the heat from a boiler making steam upon the reaction in water.

2. More than two things must react against each other; otherwise energy dissipates. Burning fuel to produce steam is futile if it's not transformed into motion. The two extra bits can hold inputs/outputs, sort of like a ballast, before moving it to the next step. Think about the chambers and pistons in a steam engine.

3. These few things need to move in concert so that they don't create too powerful a reaction, expending more energy than necessary. They need to generate just enough steam for the chambers to hold it, and only for as long as it takes for the piston to turn the crank.

4. There's an intermediate, sort of magical step that involves entropy: the period of time where the things moving around can't be converted into energy because they're re-forming into other things. This is when the cranks almost stop . . . then move again when a critical mass of steam builds up.

---

* https://en.wikipedia.org/wiki/Carnot_cycle.

5. They have to do something in the real world. Pistons turn a crank (that typically moves something else).

6. They have to return to their initial state to start again. The pistons go back to where they started at every turn of the crank.

Now let's apply this to data learning loops.

1. Data reacts with models to generate predictions.

2. Models output predictions to human beings who think about what to do with those predictions before acting on them in the real world. So, the four factors are data (fuel), models (air), people acting on the prediction (chamber and pistons), and the thing acted upon (crank).

3. Data, models, and people move in concert, mostly because nothing can move faster than the humans.

4. Entropy occurs when the human is thinking (the chamber), and her action is having an effect in the real world (the cranks turn).

5. People act on predictions, and their actions are observable.

6. The observation is data from which a model can learn and then generate a new prediction, starting the loop all over again.

Ideally, all of this happens efficiently, without dissipating energy along the way, wasting inputs. In the case of a car engine, that input is gasoline. In the case of an AI-First product, those inputs are data, an engineer's time, and customer attention.

Thinking about loops this way helps us discern a good loop from a bad loop. A good loop has ample inputs and increases entropy.

Ample inputs mean more data. Increasing entropy lets human beings do lots of things with the prediction so that it can have an effect in the real world that models can observe. Increasing entropy can also happen when humans contribute a lot of feedback. Disorder is eventually resolved by the model's having observed all the effects on the real world, digesting the feedback, and incorporating it into the models in order to run the loop again. Otherwise there's nothing more than a lot of useless output from sensors or human feedback to process. This is just an abstract analogy that may be helpful in considering how loops work. We now move to moats, a different analogy and one on which to develop the concept of a loop.

Moats Versus Loops

Traditionally, the metaphor of a castle moat described a competitive advantage. However, a moat is a static concept. Once built, it

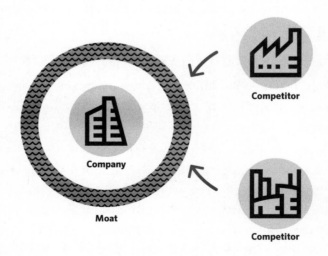

may increase or decrease in size, making it harder or easier for enemies to storm the castle, but it doesn't automatically get deeper.

The problem is that the world of business is dynamic, in that competitive forces change, and moats can change shape.

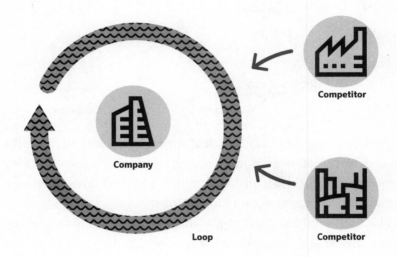

The metaphor of a moat doesn't work with DLEs. When unique data is the source of a competitive advantage—the water in the moat, so to speak—and that data is automatically increasing, at an increasing rate, thanks to the output of an intelligent system, the moat changes shape. The metaphor of a loop is more useful because it goes in the same direction with each iteration but can increase in size.

The area of the loop represents the degree of competitive advantage. This is like a moat but one that is automatically increasing in size, not just shape.

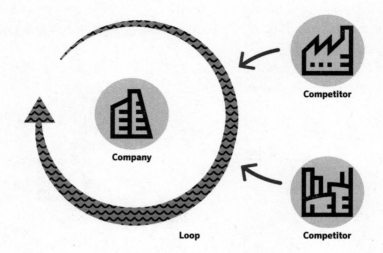

Data learning loops automatically increase in size because the value of information compounds. Everything that goes in the loop stays in the loop. Data learning loops keep all the information generated and use it to generate more information.

The loop could stop, though—for example, if the model becomes unstable, failing to learn anymore. The loop could also be supplanted if someone copies the whole thing. However, loops that have been running for a while are hard to supplant because every run of the loop adds data that can be connected to new data collected in the next run of the loop.

LIGHTING UP THE RIGHT LOOP

Data learning loops require a big investment, beyond just writing code, but the payoff is commensurate. Customers contribute to this investment with their data, but their continuing contribution depends on performance, risk to get results from the loop, and whether it will last. What follows is a guide to determining whether customers will participate in the loop and how to make it last.

Product Payoffs

Machine learning relies on probabilistic methods to model uncertainty. Probabilities don't always hold, so the models don't always work. Keep this in mind when building ML products in order to meet customers' expectations, at best, and avoid the unchecked use of ML in high-stakes situations, at worst.

Payoffs

One way to think about a product's value to a customer is to model the shape of the payoff from using that product. These payoffs are usually in the shape of a curve—*convex* or *concave*.

CONVEX VERSUS CONCAVE PAYOFFS

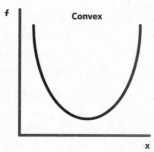
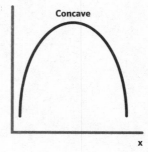

Convex payoffs represent an increase in value with use. That is, more use means more gain. Consumer applications are the most attainable example of this: it costs you almost nothing timewise to perform a Google search, and every result bears some informational value. Bad results don't hurt. (The negative segment at the start is the cost of the product.)

CONVEX PAYOFF

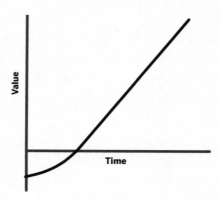

Concave payoffs represent a decrease in value. That is, more use means less gain.

CONCAVE PAYOFF

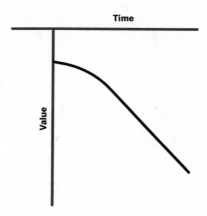

The key word here is *likely*: the shape of the curve is based on probabilities.

This seems a little abstract, but it is remarkably useful when thinking about where to apply ML—in other words, when the expected value of using the product exceeds the cost. By way of reminder, the expected value is equal to the payoff value multiplied by the probability of getting that payoff. Another way to think of this is in terms of interaction frequency. What is the average user experience of a product? If it's a one-off interaction, as with diagnosing a disease, then the denominator of the "average" in "average user experience" is 1, and so the interaction has to be perfect. That's a problem because machine learned systems aren't 100 percent accurate. Here are some examples of each type of payoff.

Convex

Marketing: AI-based marketing products deliver new leads. Even if these leads go nowhere, there may be a high upside—at negligible cost—from chasing them down. For instance, some companies can identify "anonymous" visitors to a website and, from that, produce enriched profiles to use as marketing leads and contact details for prospecting those leads. The low cost of such a product is outweighed by the high payoff of getting a new customer.

Sales: AI-based sales products prioritize leads. These tools increase the chance that the lead will close. The low cost of using these products is, again, outweighed by the high payoff of gaining a new customer.

Inventory: AI-assisted inventory management can identify gaps in stock levels in order to restock on a timely basis and therefore catch customers when they want to buy—for example, running computer vision algorithms over videos collected in grocery stores to identify out-of-stock items so that the staff can quickly restock, meaning that customers can buy more.

Concave

Scheduling: AI-based personal assistants (arguably) save time. However, the ROI calculus is a little lopsided (convex) for customers. The gains from using such a product are tricky to calculate because it's difficult to value a user's time. The losses, however, are potentially high. For example, if a scheduling bot schedules meetings, it "did the job." However, that bot might double book, causing a missed meeting with an important person. This is a costly mistake that the user ascribes to the bot.

Customer service: AI-based customer support bots can cheaply and quickly answer questions. But again, the ROI calculus is a little lopsided for customers. The gains from using such a product are dampened because the bot will answer a ticket in the most efficient way—there will be no surprise, delight, and relationship-building with customers. The losses, however, from using such a product can be high if the bot merely creates more follow-up questions for people to answer or makes a customer angry.

Picking the Product to Build

Founders, product managers, and designers must carefully consider whether a system with probabilistic assumptions will deliver what their customers need or if a deterministic system is a better choice. The answer depends on how often it needs to be right, and by how much. Deriving what customers really want and getting that from a product is often harder than building the technology itself.

Sufficient Scale

Getting to the prediction usability threshold requires a sufficient scale of data. Remember our initial formula from Chapter 1, "Defining Data Learning Effects," showing that output is a function of data:

output = function(data network effect(processed data quality(data amount))).

This means that getting output requires some data. Products without enough data to get a DLE in motion won't provide enough value to customers to encourage them to contribute more data and keep the DLE going. AI-First companies can procure enough data by ingesting customer data in bulk, partnering with complementary data sources, and using the other tactics mentioned in Chapter 4, "AI-First Teams."

Not All Data Feeds the Loop

Keep in mind that not all data contributes to a model's output. Some data is used to build a model and is then thrown out, while some is used as the input to the system, and some is put back into the system through a feedback mechanism. It's only the latter of these three that contributes to the model's output on an ongoing basis.

Training data is thrown out after use, so it doesn't accumulate in value. This data includes three separate datasets: training, validation, and holdout data. By way of reminder, training data teaches the ML algorithm predictive features. Validation data checks the predictions. Holdout data validates the prediction generated by the trained model after letting it run for a while and seeing if it matches reality.

Input data goes in and out of a system as it's used to make predictions. Validation data from the holdout group, defined above, can be used as input data. This input data later trains new models, so it is a potential asset.

Feedback data changes the system, hopefully so that it can make better predictions. This is the most proprietary data. Design products to constantly collect feedback data; for example, ask customers if the prediction was right, to correct it, or to just accept it. Feedback data is proprietary because it comes from something customers observed in the real world only after acting on the prediction made by the model. Competitors won't have those observations.

The Other Side of Scale

Loops improve with every run, as more data goes into the loop and the DLE is at work. However, as seen in the core DLE formulas, data can have limited utility beyond a certain point. Note the last part of this formula: log(economies of scale to data). This means that the increase in output from having more data is dependent on the economies of scale to data.

> percentage increase in output from more data = log (value of data network effects) + log(value of processed data to a data network) + log(economies of scale to data).

There isn't a powerful DLE—a high increase in output from more data—where there are very low economies of scale to data. This means that new entrants get to the same level of output without gathering much data, either because the value of data network effects or the value of processed data to the data network is particularly high. Such is the case when, for instance, the ML methods used to generate predictions are efficient with data, in that they don't need much data to reach the PUT. However, where there are very high economies of scale to data, it may take a lot of capital or time to build a DLE. This is a challenge but also an opportunity to build *defensibility*.

However, there are two ways this defensibility may not last: algorithmic breakthroughs or diminishing returns to scale. New entrants leveraging algorithmic breakthroughs that achieve the same level of output with less data can leapfrog incumbents. For example, contemporary Bayesian approaches to ML are effective in generating accurate predictions on small datasets. The scale effect also has limitations: even if there's an initial return to scale of data, there may be diminishing returns to data after a certain point. More data may not improve the model; the DLE may just stop. Monitor this ratio of return over cost of improvement by logging the model's improvements over the cost of harvesting more data or engineering more features for the model. Once the product yields diminishing returns, companies deliver more value to customers by gathering data to solve adjacent problems.

Minimizing Drift

Models drift if the data used to train them no longer lines up with the real world. Models trained on highly perishable data might seem to favor new entrants, but, in practice, incumbents with widely deployed systems may have the best access to fresh data in high volume. The question for the AI-First company is whether it can get enough fresh data—from customers or other sources—to minimize model drift.

Managing to reach the PUT in a highly dynamic system and then getting enough fresh data to stay at that level of accuracy generates a significant advantage over others trying to model the same system. Even if you get a prediction about delivery times right once, getting it right the second time can be very hard without up-to-the-minute data on the location of a package, weather, traffic, and other inputs. Learning the dynamics of these systems to the point of being able to predict outcomes is nigh impossible without augmentation by AI; where learning curves are perpetual, DLEs are crucial.

Prying Out the Perfect Prediction Problem

This is how it all comes together: make predictions (1) that aren't too risky to use in the real world; (2) for which there is a convex payoff in use; (3) that can get to the PUT with available data; and (4) for which there are some returns to scale of data.

Here are some questions to ask to "thread the needle."

❑ What is the degree of risk? How much money would be lost if decisions are incorrect? Would any people get hurt if this goes wrong?

❑ What is the degree of resource augmentation? How could this help customers do more with their existing work force or reduce their current head count? How could this help customers stretch the dollars invested into this activity?

❑ Is there data to train models? Is there enough to train the learning algorithm?

❑ How quickly could a new entrant reach sufficient scale of data?

❑ Are there diminishing returns to data? Does the model keep getting better, or is there a performance ceiling?

❑ Is there enough fresh, real data to keep the model from drifting? If fresh data is not already available, are there pipelines to collect that data, or will it require a significant investment in data collection methods such as deploying sensors?

❑ Is the underlying system dynamic—constantly changing—to the point where it's impossible to model without fresh data? If so, is there fresh proprietary data available?

Domains with low returns to scale of data and high potential for drift are not very defensible. New entrants can readily amass enough data to leapfrog earlier entrants. On the other hand, companies attacking problems with high returns to scale of data and low potential for drift could build a moat by acquiring new data faster than competitors and continuing to get fresh data.

	LOW POTENTIAL FOR DRIFT	HIGH POTENTIAL FOR DRIFT
LOW RETURNS TO SCALE OF DATA	Need to acquire data fast	Not defensible
HIGH RETURNS TO SCALE OF DATA	Defensible	High up-front investment

MEASURING THE MODELS

Loops are powered by the underlying predictive models, and the performance of those models can be quantified. Some of the main metrics used in ML are shown below. There are many others, and each generation of models has its own metrics, but these are the fundamental metrics that apply to many types of models.

Accuracy

Accuracy is the measure of how many predictions are correct as a fraction of all predictions made. Figuring out what's "correct" requires referencing back to the real world—the ground truth—and acquiring data on what actually happened can be challenging, especially close enough to real time in order to assess the accuracy of the model before customers get fed up with inaccuracies. That's it: when we refer to accuracy throughout this book, that's all it means. Often, this doesn't require an understanding of any mathematics—just common sense—but it can call for a little statistics or calculus.

Binary Classification

Outcomes are often binary, such as true and false. Where that's the case, accuracy is measured in a different way. There's true and false in the real world and positive and negative in the model world. The real world sees something only as true (it exists/happened) or false (it doesn't exist/didn't happen). For example, there was a cat in the frame or there was not a cat in the frame, according to verified real-world data. The model world says something was positively identified or negatively identified. There are thus four possible outcomes.

	TRUE	FALSE
Positive	True positive	False positive
Negative	True negative	False negative

True positive and false negative are when the model made a correct prediction, while true negative and false positive are where the model was incorrect.

Here's how to measure accuracy where the classification of outcomes is binary.

ACCURACY EQUATION

$$\text{Accuracy} = \frac{TP + TN}{TP + TN + FP + FN}$$

The judgment call to make is when to deem something positive *enough* to be true or negative *enough* to be false. Outcomes that are truly binary involve less of a judgment call: the pixel is either black or white, and the model output is either black or white. However, few outcomes are truly binary, so a model often has a percentage attached to its classification. Let's say that a model is 90 percent sure there's a cat in the photo. Set a threshold and deem the model to be right when it outputs a positive above a certain threshold— for example, above that 90 percent.

Receiver Operating Characteristic

The *receiver operating characteristic (ROC)* curve shows how well the model performed at different thresholds.

Set the threshold at different levels and collect the true positive rate and the false positive rate at each threshold. This is a curve plotted on *x* and *y* axes, with the *y* (vertical) axis being the true positive rate and the *x* (horizontal) axis being the false positive rate.

TRUE VERSUS FALSE POSITIVE RATE AT DIFFERENT DECISION THRESHOLDS

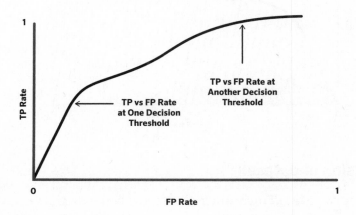

TRUE POSITIVE RATE EQUATION

$$TPR = \frac{TP}{TP + FN}$$

FALSE POSITIVE RATE EQUATION

$$FPR = \frac{FP}{FP + TN}$$

Calculate the *area under the curve (AUC)* by integrating this curve. This is the shaded part. This area gives an aggregate measure of how accurate the model was across all the different thresholds. Where the model is always correct, the AUC will be 1—the whole space—and where it is wrong, it will be 0.

AREA UNDER THE CURVE

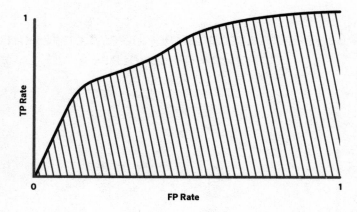

Precision and Recall

Precision and *recall* measure how effectively the model retrieves and identifies relevant results. Precision is the number of relevant data points retrieved by the model over the total number of data points. Recall is the number of relevant data points retrieved by the model over the total number of *relevant* data points. Probabilistically, precision is the probability that a randomly retrieved data point is relevant, while recall is the probability that a randomly selected, relevant data point is retrieved in a search. Measuring both is important because precision alone doesn't provide an indication of how far off the model is from capturing all of the relevant results, and recall can reach 100 percent by merely retrieving all documents.

PRECISION EQUATION

$$\text{precision} = \frac{|\{\text{relevant documents}\} \cap \{\text{retrieved documents}\}|}{|\{\text{retrieved documents}\}|}$$

RECALL EQUATION

$$\text{recall} = \frac{|\{\text{relevant documents}\} \cap \{\text{retrieved documents}\}|}{|\{\text{relevant documents}\}|}$$

Loss

Loss is the quantum of *how* right or wrong the model was in making a given prediction. Perfect predictions have zero loss, and from there, it's a question of degree. Measuring loss is useful in ML because not all outcomes are binary, and the process for improving a model is to gradually reduce loss at every iteration. Measuring loss depends on whether one is looking across a whole dataset or part of it, or expecting a lot of outliers or a fairly uniform distribution, among a multitude of other factors. Square all the losses to see if there's a regression to the mean in losses, indicating whether to change anything at all. Graph loss at different parameter weights to see if there's a point at which loss is minimized and fix the weights at that point. To find that point, get a derivative of this curve to figure out if it's getting closer (descending the curve, on a negative gradient) or farther away (ascending the curve, on a positive gradient) to ultimately know how the parameter weights get us to the minimum level of loss. This is called *gradient descent*.

GRADIENT DESCENT

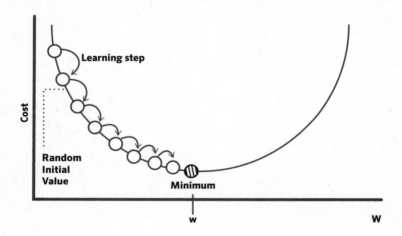

Figuring out how to make a model better in collaboration with the person building it may require going to this deeper level, yet understanding it typically involves only basic calculus.

Manual Acceptance

AI-First products can include explicit ways for customers to provide feedback on decisions—implicitly accepting or rejecting the prediction behind that decision. For example, the product can serve up a decision that there is a dangerous skin lesion in a picture, and the dermatologist using the product can agree or disagree. This is perhaps the highest single measure of predictive accuracy because the human user giving that feedback is probably applying their intuition, and that's based on all of their real-world experience and domain knowledge. This is, in many cases, more reliable than any statistical measure.

Usage Metrics

Let's not forget the basics here: the easiest way to tell if customers derive value from the product is to see how much they're using it. Usage metrics are idiosyncratic to the product, ideally measuring the core action that customers take to get value from the product, such as clicking on a search result (not just performing a search) or buying a product (not just clicking around a catalogue). The additional actions to measure for AI-First products are those that gather feedback data for the underlying models. Product managers can go through the product, noting each point at which a customer generates feedback data—explicitly or implicitly, entering it or generating it—and then measure the usage of the product around those points to figure out ways to improve usage, thus generating additional feedback data. Some users may generate more feedback data than others—**power generators** for models, just like *power users* for products—and some may generate higher-quality feedback data than others—**power teachers** in the world of DLEs. Figuring out who they are, talking to them, and building more features for them may lead to obtaining still more high-quality feedback data.

MACHINE EARNING

Businesses must eventually sustain themselves beyond external funding sources by turning profits. What's talked about less than ML itself is how one can leverage machine learned models to generate profits. This section provides profitability metrics and illuminates levers to pull that can improve those metrics.

Data learning loops bring about profit and create investment opportunities for the AI-First vendor: better predictions can lead to more automation, which lowers operating costs, which in turn means more gross profit that can be invested in research and development (models and data), leading to better predictions, and so on. Eventually the business is so profitable on a gross basis that it covers all of the operating costs and thus nets a profit.

DATA LEARNING LOOPS FOR VENDORS

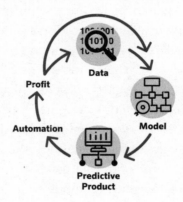

The other way to think of this is from the customer-acquisition perspective: greater prediction accuracy can lead to more automation, attracting more customers or encouraging existing customers to use the product more, thus generating more data, leading to better predictions, and so on.

Vertical Versus Horizontal

"Vertical" AI-First products present more profitability challenges than "horizontal" products. *Vertical products* apply ML to commercial or industrial data to generate a prediction of value to their

DATA LEARNING LOOPS FOR CUSTOMERS

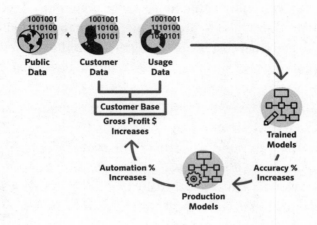

customers. I'll give you an example: a vertical product that gathers data from machines on a production line and uses it to train a model that predicts when the production line might fail, so that customers can avoid costly failures. Another example is amassing data from large sets of product images and using it to train a model that recognizes those products in a warehouse or store, so that customers can avoid costly stockouts. Horizontal products include tools for ML engineers and data scientists across different verticals.

The economics of such businesses are quite different, with vertical businesses needing to solve a specific process problem for their customers and horizontal businesses needing to solve a general process problem. Vertical businesses need to vertically integrate around the customer problem, figuring out all the things that a customer needs to solve their whole problem. This can involve integrating with one specific data source owned by a customer, building them a workflow product that outputs the prediction, and instituting features that work for the specific user at their company. Horizontal businesses need to generalize their solution so that it works for those working in companies in different verticals. This can involve integrating with lots of different data sources, workflow products, and communication tools. AI-First companies building horizontal products tend to present fewer profitability challenges because the marginal cost of delivering those products is low, and thus the economics of such businesses tends to be similar to that of traditional software companies.

This framework is no different for AI-First companies than it is for traditional software companies. Vertical, traditional software businesses need to build all sorts of integrations, features, and flows for those in their industry. For instance, Veeva Systems is a world-class vertical software company that integrates with a multitude of products used by medical professionals in order to provide features such as clinical data management and workflows that make regulatory submissions more efficient for their customers. Horizontal, traditional software businesses need to build integrations, features, and flows for those across industries. Salesforce, the first-rate horizontal software company, has an entire cloud platform through which different vendors can integrate, a marketplace of applications that offer industry-specific features, and flexible API that allows customers to build their own workflows across applications.

Profit

Here's a quick reminder of the difference between gross, operating, and net profit:

Revenue
Less: cost of goods sold (COGS)
Gross Profit
Less: operating expenses
Operating Profit
Less: interest and taxes
Net Profit

Unit Analysis

The first way to think about measuring profitability is on a unit basis. Unit analysis is simply that: picking a unit and analyzing its profitability. The relevant unit of profitability for every business is different and often depends on the business model. For example, building something that reduces a machine's energy usage might mean charging as a percentage of energy savings; thus, the unit would be a piece of machinery, and the basis of measurement would be energy usage.

The business model may be based on a set of improvements and in a multitiered pricing model, so often it makes sense to just pick the customer as the unit. That means allocating all the revenues and expenses associated with that customer to the unit. Allocating the revenues is straightforward—that's just billings per customer—but allocating the expenses often involves tracking all the sales, presales engineering, data integration, product integration, training, customer-specific feature engineering, customer-specific model training, customer success, customer support, and other costs to the unit. With both the revenue and expenses for the unit, calculate gross profit for the unit.

	2020 (Actual)
Average price per unit	$0.10
– labor cost	$0.05
– QA cost	$0.02
Contribution margin (CM)	$0.03
– services cost	$0.01
Gross margin (GM)	$0.02 (20 percent)

The goal is to increase the unit's gross profit. That entails, first, profitably providing the product as measured by the *contribution margin*, then making the customer profitable on a gross basis, accounting for the cost of providing the services necessary to deliver the product.

Calculating net profit for the unit is far more complicated because it's usually not possible to allocate the costs of everything—from research and development to office space—to a specific customer. We cover this below.

Input Cost Analysis

Every business uses inputs to obtain outputs. Companies that output predictions tend to spend money on data as inputs. Analyzing the cost of the data inputs is fertile ground for generating profit.

Data is either new or old. New data comes from labeling; old data comes from a pipe.

Data Labeling

Data labeling is done by expert and nonexpert people or by machines. Expert humans are employed to label things that require special knowledge to identify, such as a bone in the body. Experts with such special knowledge can be expensive to hire, so these labels cost more on a per-label basis. Nonexpert humans are employed to identify and label things that don't require special knowledge, such as a chair or box. Nonexperts tend to be flexible in how they work and are available for hire on various platforms, the most well-known being Amazon's Mechanical Turk. Machines can label things without help from us. The degree to which they can do that depends on the techniques used and the data to label.

The first metric is labeling cost per unit of value. This is clear-cut when outsourcing labeling to a vendor—the cost is whatever the vendor bills—but less so when labelers are employed by customers, or staff software engineers pitch in to label data during the training step, or when something breaks. With the latter situation, figure out how the staff spends its time preparing data for training ML models, and allocate the time used for labeling to an input cost for a given unit of value, such as a customer's project.

A second metric is the split between expert and nonexpert labeling, and how it is changing over time. Assuming that experts are more expensive than nonexperts and that we have to label the same amount of data over time, we want to figure out how to shift the balance of labeling work from experts to nonexperts. The precursor is the *agreement rate* between experts and nonexperts. That is, if nonexperts agree with the experts a high percentage of the time, start shifting more work to the nonexperts and achieving the same accuracy of the labels and thus performance of the model.

Using machines is probably going to be cheaper than hiring people, so it's worth exploring techniques such as active learning and forms of semisupervised learning, such as generative adversarial networks.

Finally, explore using machines to generate synthetic data, even if lots of data still needs labeling. Synthetic data generation systems can generate both the data and associated labels in one package.

Data Pipes

Getting old data from customers involves building pipes from customers' data to ML systems. Those pipes take time to build, but the cost of this engineering time or outsourcing this to a systems integrator can be amortized over the life of the customer relationship because those pipes (usually) hold in place once built. Attributing the cost of engineering time to a unit of value, such as a customer project, helps to figure out if that customer is profitable.

Sometimes it's not as simple as building a pipe—for example, manually inputting data.

One way to reduce the costs of building these pipes is to build software to automate integration, train lower-level engineers to carry out data integration, choosing to work only with customers that have more common types of data stores (and thus cheap or even free pipes), or outsourcing.

Research Cost Analysis

Research and development (R & D) budgets can be significant in technology companies. The cost of building software that could be used by all potential customers is often considered to be R & D rather than a cost of goods sold (COGS), and some large, established companies allocate 25 percent of their capital to R & D. Classifying expenses as R & D rather than COGS affects net and gross profits, respectively.

The classification of expenses related to software development is difficult and often controversial because it's hard to say which features and code maintenance tasks are required for maintenance, to launch a customer, or land potential customers.

AI-First companies have expenses beyond the development of software features, such as manually tuning a model's features or cleaning up data, that are arguably R & D if the features can be transposed onto a global model that works across customers or if incoming data improves the model's overall performance.

So, how does one manage R & D expenses in an AI-First company? Break down the R & D efforts to see what's working. ML researchers and engineers work on improving the performance of models used by all customers or customizing a model to work well for a particular customer. Earning more in the latter case is a matter of, on the one side of the ledger, making sure to charge customers for custom feature development and, on the other side, completing that development in a short enough time to earn a 100 percent or more margin on an engineer's effective hourly rate in order to at least cover her "all-in" cost to the company. Earning more in the former case is a more difficult task. The goal of figuring out what's working is to make sure that they are indeed working on features that are likely to improve the global performance of the model. This seems challenging, but it just requires applying the scientific method. That is, form a hypothesis about what effort—

adding a feature, adding some data, and so forth—will yield what result, be it improved accuracy, stability, and so on. Then perform the experiment and follow up diligently. For example, when trying to recognize the brand on a cereal box 98 percent of the time using supervised learning, experiment with training the model on labeled images of cereal boxes taken in low light or at an odd angle, then run the retrained model against real-world examples to see if accuracy improved across the board. Sometimes domain experts have learned heuristics—things gleaned on the job—that provide shortcuts with experiments by just hardcoding in a feature such as: "Whenever we see that the bottle cap is 1 millimeter off, we know that the next step in bottle production will break, so stop the line." We don't need a model to learn to make that prediction if someone learned it over and over again in her career.

CONCLUSION:
FLYWHEELS FIRST

Measuring the right thing causes you to *do* the right thing. I see companies that try to put AI first fail because they ultimately chase a goal that's not reinforcing the core DLE. Seeing the power of data learning loops in action instills that understanding. More prosaically, the accounting systems for AI-First companies are nascent—the industry hasn't settled on appropriate rules—so I've worked with companies to develop our own that make sure we build sustainable businesses. I've seen those that use the metrics explored in this chapter build the most valuable companies.

Thinking of something as a dynamic system aids understanding as to what is going on when it inevitably changes. DLEs quickly start looping—self-reinforcing with every repetition—after the flywheel spins them up. However, sometimes it's hard to get that flywheel spinning because the risk of adopting AI is insurmountable, expectations of its performance too high, available data to train it too little, and data to keep it up-to-date unavailable. Pick the right problem to solve using the frameworks and metrics in this section, and you might just get that flywheel going.

PLAYBOOK

- **The motion of a DLE is looping.** Learning is a process that happens in loops: observe something, learn from it, act on it, and observe the effect. DLEs are also a process that happens in loops: get data, put it into a model, output a prediction, and observe the accuracy.

- **Moats are the wrong metaphor.** Moats are an accumulation of assets that form a barrier, but barriers can be broken down and those assets taken away from you. DLEs accumulate not only data assets but also lessons.

- **Loops grow and grow.** Data learning loops grow automatically, changing in shape and size as they automatically accumulate lessons with every run—with every repetition of the learning process.

- **Data learning loops are powerful because they endogenously generate assets, capabilities, and information.** Data, process, and lessons are automatically created by intelligent systems with every run of the loop.

- **There are good loops and bad loops.** A good loop has ample data inputs and lets entropy increase by letting people do lots of things with the prediction so that it can have an effect in the real world that models can observe. Let customers do something with the prediction, collect more information for the models, and learn more.

(continued)

- **Consider the payoff of solving the problem.** Founders, product managers, and designers must carefully think through whether a system with probabilistic assumptions will deliver what customers need, or if a deterministic system is a better choice, based on the cost of being wrong.

- **Realize the bar.** The PUT is the minimum level of performance required to justify adoption. Figure out what customers expect, what is achieved, and make sure they line up to deliver a prediction that's accurate enough to be useful for customers in the real world.

- **Get to sufficient scale.** Assess what is accessible and whether you can reach sufficient scale of data or leave models needing more data.

- **Not all data feeds the loop.** Some data is used to build a model but is then thrown out, some is used as the input to the system, and some is put back into the system through a feedback mechanism. It's only the latter of these three that forms the basis of a competitive advantage.

- **Watch for drift.** Fresh training data must be acquired at the same rate that the environment is changing. Without that data, the model may start diverging from reality.

- **Consider all the dimensions of performance when choosing a problem to solve.** Domains with low returns to scale of data and high potential for drift are not very defensible. On the other hand, companies attacking problems with high returns to scale of data and low potential for drift are defensible.

- **Measure the models.** Accuracy, binary classification, ROC, precision/recall, and loss can indicate whether a model is working to deliver predictions and how it's getting closer to reaching accuracy.

- **Track costs on a unit basis.** Figure out the core unit delivered to customers and measure both revenue and expenses for that unit to initially assess the profit potential of an AI-First company. Then layer on labeling, data pipeline, data collection, and research and development costs to arrive at an accurate gross profit number.

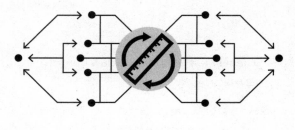

EIGHT

AGGREGATING ADVANTAGES

AI-First companies employ many of the same strategic frameworks as other companies, but they build DLEs that can capture enough information about a process to automate it, ultimately reducing costs. These cost savings unlock options for managers of AI-First companies.

1. Keep prices the same:
   - take the difference as profits;
   - reinvest the profits in the technology behind DLEs, automating more and further reducing costs; and
   - reinvest the profits in the business to vertically integrate or re-position it to get more data.
2. Lower prices, leveraging the gains from automation to pursue the following and thus be in a favorable position to beat competitors in existing markets or enter new markets:
   - price discrimination;
   - disruption; and
   - aggregation.

AGGREGATING ADVANTAGES

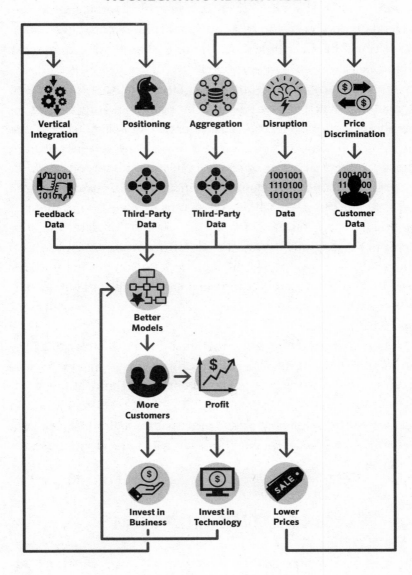

This chapter walks through the five strategies at the top of the diagram above—*vertical integration, positioning through standardization, data aggregation, disruptive market entry, or price discrimination based on data contribution*—that generate more data to feed models, grow the DLE, and attract more customers. Managers can either distribute these profits to shareholders or reinvest in business, technology, or strategies to further grow the DLE.

After working through the strategies above, this chapter also considers how DLEs give AI-First companies an edge against incumbents. Getting data from customers' existing databases, transforming it into new products, and integrating services around those products takes customers from the incumbent software providers. Companies that capture a critical mass of customers from incumbents can make whole ecosystems revolve around them by setting industry standards for storing and moving data. The concepts in the diagram above—disruption, aggregation, and vertical integration—allowed new entrants to subordinate incumbents over the last few decades. Applying these concepts on top of DLEs builds a whole stack of long-term, sustainable, and powerful competitive advantages.

Before diving in, remember that the prerequisite to aggregating any of the following advantages is putting AI first. Strategy is about making trade-offs in order to build competitive advantages. AI-First companies trade off capital, time, and resources to build DLEs. Only once they have data, processing capabilities, *and* data network effects—a DLE—can they aggregate other competitive advantages.

TRADITIONAL FORMS

Business strategy textbooks tend to break down competitive advantage into two top-level categories: supply and demand. This is useful vocabulary when communicating with those in the business world. Within supply, there's consolidation into inputs, processes, and scale. Within demand, there's consolidation into brand, switching, and scale. The existing vocabulary of competitive advantage maps to AI-First companies.

On the supply side, AI-First companies aggregate advantages by:

- getting privileged access to valuable data, a key **input** to AI;

- developing a **process** to turn data into information, reduce computation costs, or improve collaboration among ML researchers, engineers, and data scientists; and

- training predictive models on large volumes of data or consolidating predictive models across customers to get increasing returns to **scale**.

On the demand side, AI-First companies aggregate advantages by:

- building a strong **brand** around trust in managing data, reliability in delivering accurate predictions, or excellent service upon implementation;

- creating **switching** costs through data storage standards, ecosystems of complementary products, and long-term customer contracts; and

- designing a product that gets more useful as more users join the network around the product to get increasing returns to **scale**.

Otherwise, AI-First companies might aggregate government-granted advantages such as exclusive licenses to work with government data, patents on their models, or subsidies for providing predictions that allow society to plan well and function better.

VERTICAL INTEGRATION

The best products in the world are made by vertically integrated businesses: Apple's hardware to software; Amazon's warehouses to websites; and, back in the nineteenth century, industrialist Andrew Carnegie's mines to mills. Famous economists such as Ronald Coase and entrepreneurs like Michael Dell, founder of Dell Technologies, espoused the benefits of vertical integration. Providing everything a customer needs in one package allows for quality control, deep relationships, and better pricing.

There is another, major benefit for AI-First companies: capturing more data from customers using the products on site, every day. This constant stream of fresh data keeps models up-to-date, accurate, and in tune with the real world.

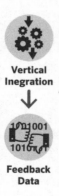

Vertical Inegration

Feedback Data

Vertical integration can accelerate adoption of new technologies. AI is a relatively new technology with idiosyncratic barriers to adoption: serious consequences, such as missing a medical diagnosis; value that's hard to calculate, such as time savings for a security analyst; and high resource requirements, such as engineers with the technical skills necessary to train an ML system. Going to a customer with a complete, vertically integrated AI-First solution that replaces software they use already makes for an easier sales process.

Indeed, there are many AI-First companies that vertically integrate. For instance, hedge funds get their own data, build their own models, and make their own trades; they do not build the models and then let others use the predictions to make trades. Advertising platforms figure out the best customers to target and then sell the ads; they don't sell the targeting models to other websites. New age consumer finance apps price the risk of offering loans and then make those loans; they don't sell the loan pricing models to banks.

And AI is moving fast. Ten years ago, the barrier to entry was high because getting AI to work at all was difficult. Today there are online libraries of code to borrow, open-source (freely available, distributable and modifiable) software, facile frameworks to use, competent consulting firms to engage, and well-trained people to hire. Indeed, many of the big technology companies are giving away basic AIs, ready to run on anyone's data, for free. Data and AI capabilities aren't enough. In the mid-2010s, it was possible to get ahead by training basic AIs on proprietary data. Today methods such as *one-shot learning*, *generative adversarial networks*, and *probabilistic programming* are good for getting models to a high degree of accuracy with relatively little data. Scale isn't enough. Combining scale of data, processing capabilities, and network effects to build a DLE is the way forward, and building all three may involve vertical integration.

What You Do

Vertical integration entails taking on and solving the *business* problem for a customer rather than just the *technical* problem—delivering not just a product but a complete solution; doing the whole job to be done. Here are some examples of what a vertically integrated company might provide:

- answer emails from customers instead of offering up suggested responses to agents tasked with responding to emails (We'll use this example throughout this section);

- serve up text in multiple languages on websites and marketing platforms instead of giving tools to language translators; and

- run an insurance company instead of helping an insurance company process claims more efficiently.

Complete solutions have many parts to them, as illustrated by the following pyramid.

Consider Alexa, the Amazon personal assistant. Going from bottom to top, these are the steps taken to bring it to life:

- financed it with internal capital;

- developed it using the Amazon Web Services computing and data infrastructure;

- collected data from early users of the product and ancillary, spoken word datasets;

- prepared that data internally without letting it leave the company, partly for privacy reasons;

- hired its own people to label snippets of voice files;

- built its own voice recognition models;

- used its own monitoring systems, again, through Amazon Web Services;

- monitored usage internally;

- built the speaker that sits in your home;

- distributed the speaker directly to customers with supporting setup tools (through mobile applications) to implement as they wish—such as connected to other speakers or as a stand-alone device; and

- got usage data to train the models and update the product over the Internet.

VERTICAL INTEGRATION FOR AI-FIRST COMPANIES

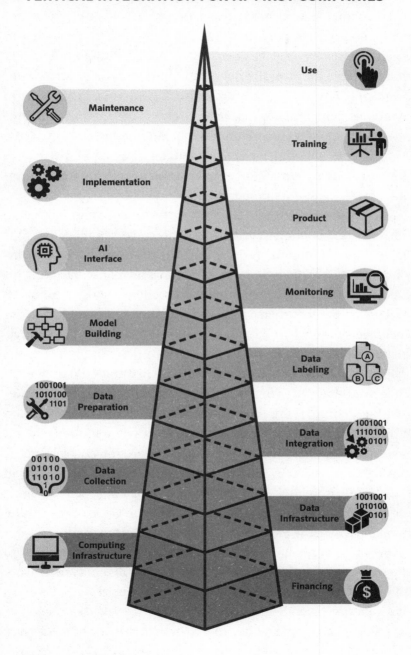

Alexa is a completely vertically integrated product.

The choice is whether to serve up predictions through other companies or go to the next level by serving them up through proprietary software, services, and other nonsoftware products. For example, that may require devising a *customer relationship management (CRM)* system to log phone calls with sales targets on top of models that predict which sales targets to call, or an email template design tool on top of models that automatically segment the email list into different types of customers who may like to receive different-looking emails, or support ticket logging on top of automated response generation models.

That's just the software. Going above technology and through to the real world is where vertical integration involves allocating capital to implementation, training, and other functions. This may include hiring people to handle exceptions by manually acting on predictions or directly dealing with customers. Those employees probably cost more than computers, but they can give 100 percent coverage—even when the model is wrong—of recognizing things, making calls, or writing emails.

Finally, let's go back to the base of the pyramid. Financing AI-First companies presents a unique opportunity for vertical integration, guaranteeing that AI works by covering the cost when it breaks. Providing this guarantee means losing money when it breaks but also profiting when it works; for example, covering the cost of loans priced by an AI that eventually default but taking all the revenue from those loans as interest. Providing such a guarantee often requires more funding to cover the costs of the model breaking while it's still learning. Venture capital is a funding option before there's enough data to show that the models are working to price risk well, but it's expensive. Other forms of equity capital are an option for companies building AI within existing businesses that generate revenue unrelated to pricing the risk. Debt becomes available when there's a track record of both the machine learning and business model working: correctly predicting a risk, under-writing it, and getting paid back. Ultimately, AI-First companies will have enough cash on their own balance sheet to cover the costs when the model is wrong—underwriting the risk—and thus get to keep all the profits, without paying any of them to outside shareholders or debt holders as interest. Vertically integrating to the point of self-financing a customer guarantee allows AI-First companies to keep all the profits from getting it right.

What You Gain

Building the services, integrations, teams, and technology around a vertically integrated offering can be both hard and expensive. There is more to build and more problems to solve. However, there are three major benefits: more data, profit, and revenue.

More Data

Providing the services that sit on top of AI models allows for collection of data, metadata, and *heuristics*—the lessons that come from doing the task to be automated—directly from customers.

Vertically integrating at the software (product) level allows for observing directly the effect of predictions as they're actioned in the real world, generating more data to feed back into models so that the next predictions are more accurate. Observations come from within the product, as users click buttons or fill out forms—see if they accept, modify, or reject the AI's output. For example, when a customer support system automatically generates a response that's approved and sent, then the model was "correct." If that response is edited before sending, the model was at least partially wrong, but it can make adjustments such as learning to not use a certain word next time and seeing if the response is acceptable. Observations also come from outside the product, as sensors pick up images or sounds. Owning the product that people use every day and the sensors that feed data into that product demands owning the data and using it to improve the models.

Vertically integrating at the people (services) level generates domain expertise that's useful when developing ideas for making better predictions and labeling data. Ideas for making better predictions come from the people hired to be onsite with customers every day, observing what they do and talking to those with lots of experience in their industry. Often, just asking someone who's done the same job for twenty years what he or she thinks is the one thing that's predictive of something else can shortcut building many ML models.

I'll give you an example: when integrating a customer support system, ask tenured *customer support agents* for something they say that typically elicits a positive response from customers. Inserting that phrase into automatically generated responses means the system is more likely to positively resolve customers' issues. Or, add a button to the customer support system that agents click to label an email as "sensitive" if they think the customer who wrote it is particularly angry and needs attention in short order: labeled data to train the ML models to prioritize responses. Vertically integrating domain experts by hiring them to implement systems yields better ideas and better data to improve models.

More Revenue

Companies that take on risk get paid for that risk if they price it well. The most pointed example, investment firms, price the risk that a company will earn a return on invested capital by using the capital to build a product, design a profitable business model, and maintain profit margins by virtue of some form of competitive advantage. Investors price each of those component risks—product and market, business and sales, and competition—and are rewarded when they price them better than others. That is, they get paid for figuring out before other investors if a company can deploy capital to reduce the risk of building a product, finding customers in a market, signing business deals, hiring good salespeople, and staying ahead of the competition. Investment companies are among the biggest in the world because their profits from pricing risk compound for as long as they don't get it totally wrong. AI-First companies can scale revenue in the same way if they create a business model based on pricing risks.

What's more, AI-First companies can get paid for taking on the risk that the AI works. Customers can specify the thing they want to predict, the level of accuracy that makes the prediction usable, and what getting it right will yield. However, customers can't control whether the model delivers that level of accuracy, and, consequently, whether they will get a return on their investment in AI. Customers don't want to take on the risk that the AI works. Continuing our example, it only makes sense to pay for the product if it costs less than the current cost of answering customer support emails *and* maintains the same quality, as measured by customer satisfaction scores. Paying for an AI-First product that automatically generates acceptable answers (as measured by customer satisfaction scores) will bring about a positive return on investment for the customer if the cost of resolution per ticket is lower than the current cost. The customer gets the same result at a lower cost, the AI-First company earns more profits as automation increases, and cost per resolution goes lower than what the customer pays.

Let's compare this to traditional software business models. There's more certainty in building and delivering software features than there is in delivering accurate predictions. Customers specify the software features that will save or generate money for them, the vendor builds a product with those features, delivers it, and gets paid. For instance, when you buy Zendesk, the cloud-based customer support system, you know what you're paying and which features you're getting. The customer controls whether the software delivers the features he wants and thus knows that he will see a return on his investment. He gets a good return if the product does

ROI-BASED PRICING FOR AI-FIRST COMPANIES

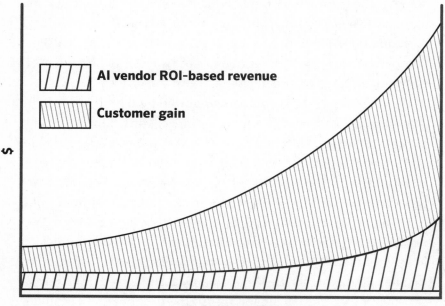

what he thought it would do and a poor return if it doesn't do as advertised, or if his staff just doesn't want to use the product. The deterministic nature of specifying software features allows for relatively deterministic pricing: fixed on a known basis of value, whether paid up front or on a subscription basis. AI-First products carry both the risks that come with traditional software—development, adoption, and integration—along with the additional risk that the prediction might be wrong. But this risk creates an opportunity: get paid for being right, thus generating a return on investment for customers.

The goal of *ROI-based pricing* is sharing in the value delivered to customers. The first challenge is figuring out metrics that represent customer value to use as the basis of pricing. These metrics are idiosyncratic to the product and customer. For example, an AI that understands the content of a user's technical support email and generates a response to the email effectively reduces the time and cost of responding to such emails. Non-ROI-based pricing could be a monthly software fee for running the system that generates these responses, while ROI-based pricing could include a share of the time and cost savings. Generally, software companies capture 10 percent to 30 percent of the return they generate. Under this model, more acceptable responses lead to more savings and more revenue for the AI-First vendor.

The diagram above shows a business model based on the percentage of ROI. The AI-First vendor collects a share of the customer's returns from automation. From a customer's perspective the percentage of ROI lines up with the returns from automation.

Vertical integration is, again, an important consideration. Price according to ROI means delivering that ROI, and that often requires running the entire system. Using the example above, that means:

- pulling tickets from a ticket management system;

- delivering the auto-generated responses back into the system;

- training the customer support representatives to approve tickets; and

- correcting auto-generated responses that aren't good enough to send as they are.

Each of these steps costs money and may add up to more than the cost of building a whole new customer support system.

Controlling the costs of data integration, delivery, training, and support determines profitability. For example, selling the customer a complete solution and then providing it cheaply by automating integration with reusable database connectors, standardized online training materials delivered at zero marginal cost, and comprehensive support documentation without support staff may allow for greater profit. Charging customers based on ROI is a unique opportunity for AI-First companies to earn more revenue as the system becomes more effective. However, it requires taking on the risk of providing the product at a low-enough cost to earn a profit.

More Profit

The reasons to vertically integrate center on the incremental gross profit available in each piece of the pyramid and customer capabilities. For example, it might cost 50 cents to deliver a prediction through an *application programming interface (API)*—a structured way for software to communicate with other pieces of software—for which customers pay $1 per "call"—a 50 percent gross margin. However, customers may not have software developers on staff capable of using that API. Customers, in this case, need an interface through which to receive the predictions and training to understand how to use that interface, which may cost an extra $1 to build and deliver. Customers can get a lot of value out of the predictions and pay $5 for something that costs $1.50 to deliver—a 70 percent gross margin. Ascending the pyramid of vertical integration is a profitable move for the AI-First vendor.

PRICE DISCRIMINATION

Figuring out what to charge customers is a perpetual challenge, and one that revolves around aligning perception of value with reality. Pricing provides an indication of differentiation, as customers will pay a lot for something they can't get anywhere else. Pricing strategy involves considerations of revenue quality, growth, profitability, product, marketing, and sales. AI-First companies also incorporate data strategy alongside pricing strategy. The following is a list of ways to price AI-First products.

Contributing

Data is generally valuable to an AI-First company, to make predictive models better either for a specific customer or for all customers. In the latter case, customers effectively form a coalition of data contributors that enjoy the benefits of better decisions thanks to the aggregate data advantage of the coalition. However, some customers will not want to share their data with others in the coalition, even if aggregated and kept anonymous. Given that these customers effectively prevent the model from improving and thus the business's ability to charge other customers more, they may be charged more.

Using

Transactional pricing—getting paid more as customers increase usage—is key to growing with customers. *Usage-based pricing* commonly looks like charging on a per-user, or per "seat," basis. However, this might not work well for AI-First products because it discourages customers from adding more users, thus reducing the amount of usage data coming back into the system. Further, charging on a per-user basis may put a ceiling on the total revenue opportunity: if the AI-First product makes a company's staff more efficient, then the company will need less staff over time and thus pay for fewer users.

The volume of data and predictions is the basis of value for AI-First products. Pricing based on data and prediction volume can allow for growth because volume isn't limited by usage. Customers may be concerned that they will use the product far more than anticipated and get stuck with an unexpectedly high bill, but this can be mitigated by usage discounts; different pricing schemes, such as a three-part tariff; and other mechanisms that incentivize usage, increase revenue, and provide certainty at the same time.

Updating

Regularly updated models can be distributed to customers through an online, cloud-based system. Charging customers upon each update cycle may be possible where the update comes with improved accuracy, reliability, or quality. Setting up an interface for customers to understand the differences between the old model and the updated model could make it obvious that the upgrade is valuable. Giving away an example of the updated model's output can entice customers to buy it. Upon purchase, customers can get updated models through a cloud system or manually upload them to their own on-premise computing system.

Features

Companies have long set pricing based on features. Single products evolve into product lines with distinct feature sets over time. AI-First companies can charge customers more the same way that software companies do: for different features, interfaces, integrations, formats, support levels, latencies, speeds, and compatibilities. The second way that AI-First companies can charge more is specific to AI: for different model features that predict different types of events, whether for a single customer to predict a specific event or for a feature that predicts events relevant to a whole segment of customers.

Delivering features in a way that allows the vendor to turn them on when customers pay for them depends on control of the delivery mechanism—a Web interface, for instance. This is one of the many ways in which pricing and product strategy interact: vertically integrated products allow for complete control of feature delivery and thus pricing according to features.

AI-FIRST DISRUPTION

According to the influential business theorist Clay Christensen's theory of disruption, spelled out in his 1997 book *The Innovator's Dilemma*,* new entrants can appropriate customers from incumbent suppliers by selling a specialized product to a niche segment of customers at a fraction of the cost of the incumbent's product. These new entrants can then build market share by selling additional products to those customers. The core assumptions here are that it's possible to identify customers that don't need all the features of the incumbent's product and to produce a more specialized, higher-quality product that costs significantly less. Discovering a niche and creating a more specialized product is an exercise in customer development and product design. This is where DLEs come into play.

Disruption

↓

1001001
1110100
1010101

Data

---

* Clayton Christensen, *The Innovator's Dilemma* (Boston: Harvard Business Review Press, 2016).

First, DLEs allow for lower prices. For example, intelligent systems that automate various steps in the drug development process by searching for all possible chemical combinations ultimately reduce the cost of producing a drug. Lower production costs allow for lower prices, and lower prices can attract customers away from competitors. This is the first phase of AI-First disruption.

Second, DLEs are the basis of features of higher-quality products such as personalization and insight generation. Incumbents often undervalue such advanced features because they view their customer base as not needing the higher-quality product, while AI-First companies can initially provide a lower-quality product at a lower price and then gradually improve the product as DLEs allow for better personalization, more accurate insight generation, or more complete automation. For example, advertising platforms such as Google initially sold ads for less than the cost of website banners but now charge more because the platforms can serve up personalized ads that generate high-quality leads for advertisers. This is the second-phase of AI-First disruption, where profit comes from selling higher-quality (and higher-priced) products.

Third, DLEs lead to the creation of products that cater to the most demanding use case: complete automation. AI-First companies own the new markets for automation solutions, leaving incumbents to wither in old markets. This is the third and final phase of AI-First disruption.

PHASES OF AI-FIRST DISRUPTION

PHASE	DESCRIPTION
1	Take customers from incumbents by selling a specialized product to a niche segment of customers, at a fraction of the cost of the incumbent's general product—because DLEs afford a lower cost of production.
2	Charge customers more for novel, AI-based features such as personalization, insight generation, and automation.
3	Create new products that provide complete automation to the most demanding customers.

AI-FIRST AGGREGATION[*]

The large amount of data flowing freely around the world creates an opportunity: aggregate that data, curate it with intelligent systems, distribute it widely to generate more data, and so on.

Aggregation

Third-Party Data

The opportunity to aggregate arises as we generate lots of data. The low transaction costs on the Internet mean it's easier to start

---

[*] Ben Thompson, "Defining Aggregators," Stratchery, accessed September 26, 2017, https://stratchery.com/2017/defining-aggregators.

using products—just enter a credit card number online—so people adopt more products and generate more data. The low distribution costs afforded by the Internet—just download the app—make it easier to sell products, allowing broad appeal and the collation of more usage data. The low marginal costs afforded by the Internet—cloud computing is cheap—allow cheap serving of products to customers online. This all leads to more customers using more products and generating more data.

When there's a lot of something, the value moves from generating more of it to discovery and curation of it. Lots of data in a bucket isn't a product, but information can be a product. The big-data era gave us some products to store, curate, and discover data in a manual way. AI can automatically curate all this data and help us discover what's relevant to the decisions we have to make. AI turns data into products.

Below you'll find the characteristics of AI-First aggregators:

- **Direct relationship with customers.** AI-First aggregators generate predictions that customers use to make decisions every day. Incumbents are the *system of record* that sits behind the AI-First product, just as a database sits behind a software application. Customers don't touch the database unless something breaks. For example, you don't deal with the company that owns the rights to movies, catalogues them, and distributes them around the world; you just click Play on what Netflix suggests watching next.

- **Zero marginal costs to serve customers.** AI-First aggregators see the cost of production go down as automation goes up. Incumbents scale by manually adding features and services to their offerings. For instance, offline publications need to have a translator go through every page and then reprint it, whereas online publications can run their articles through an automated language translation product to deliver the same article to more customers around the world.

- **Zero distribution costs.** AI-First aggregators get products to customers by integrating with or piggybacking on products that customers already use. For example, an AI-First application that gets tickets from the software program JIRA (developed by the Australian software company Atlassian Corporation) and learns how to route those tickets to the right engineers can both aggregate data and sell through the Atlassian marketplace. Incumbents, however, cannot piggyback so they have to spend money on sales and marketing to get their products to customers.

- **Zero transaction costs.** AI-First aggregators operate their systems on another vendor's infrastructure. Incumbents are effectively the database from which the AI-First product pulls data. A good example is a software application that plugs into Salesforce, the cloud-based CRM. Applications can plug into and run within the Salesforce application, pulling data and processing functions on the computing infrastructure running Salesforce, effectively reducing the marginal cost of transacting data in the AI-First product to zero.

Aggregation theory explains the current market power of companies such as Netflix but also the potential for even more market power going to AI-First companies. The streaming entertainment service has a critical mass of customers (demand) encouraging the production of content (supply), with the additional content attracting more customers, and so on, in a positively self-reinforcing loop. AI-First aggregators have the potential to build a more rapidly self-reinforcing loop because their customers are both the demand and supply sides of this equation. Essentially, a critical mass of customers (demand) can generate enough data for an AI to generate increasingly accurate predictions. In turn, the predictions' greater accuracy encourages more usage from those same customers, and so on. Customers generate enough data to kick off the flywheel in the AI, which then self-generates just enough data to increase the accuracy of the system and thus encourage more usage, in a rapidly self-reinforcing loop. This allows AI-First companies to build market power fast.

Integrating Incumbents

Software needs to integrate with existing workflows in order to be useful. AI-First aggregators reverse the direction of software integration to take incumbents' customers.

- **Incumbents integrate backward,** building a workflow tool for customers to use every day, then putting data from that workflow into a database.

- **AI-First companies integrate forward,** obtaining data from a database and building an intelligent system for customers to use every day.

AI-First aggregation is distinct from vertical integration: aggregation is about data and gets more distribution; vertical integration is about data, services, infrastructure, interfaces, etc., and increases profit. In addition, AI-First aggregation facilitates the development of new products that aggregate the data flowing across the Internet, subordinating incumbent products by sitting on top of them, pulling data from them, and then integrating around and selling through them.

Incumbents Integrated Backward

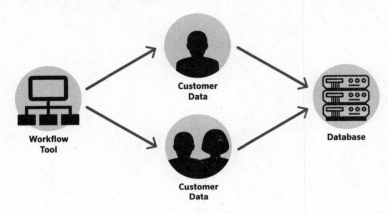

AI-First Companies Integrate Forward

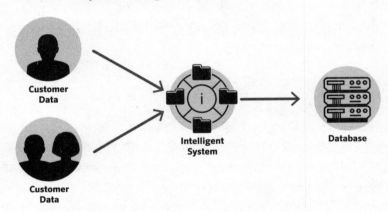

POSITIONING

The history of the software industry is full of stories about deeply embedding products in a customer's environment to protect against switching to a competitor's product. This section takes lessons from the broader technology industry and applies them to AI-First products, writing a new framework for embedding products in three layers of an industry: storage, standards, and ecosystem.

Incidentally, this section of the book may also provide those pur-chasing AI-First products with a list of items to flag in vendor contracts.

Positioning

↓

Third-Party Data

Here are the ways in which AI-First products store core assets, set the standard, catalyze an ecosystem, build a brand, and move first to capture value.

Storage

Managing data storage embeds AI-First products: for example, by offering a powerful image search tool but only to customers who agree to store all of their images in your database, or owning a sen-sor that captures and stores data. However, storing customer data involves negotiating data rights. This is a somewhat spectral con-sideration of whether to get (1) one large customer, on more re-strictive terms, with a critical mass of data to train a model to high accuracy and then quickly capturing the customers that make up the rest of the market on more permissive terms; or (2) many smaller customers, on more permissive terms, that have a critical mass of data, in aggregate, to train a model to high accuracy.

This choice depends on the data dynamics of the market: whether one or few customers have a critical mass of data. Go after one customer if they have critical mass and will sign a deal with workable data rights, otherwise go after many customers.

Storing models, for example, by requiring that they be uploaded to a cloud service, can also embed AI-First products. That is, models must be uploaded to a cloud service. This is similar to how most cloud-based software vendors manage the storage and serving of a product.

Standardization

Setting the standards by which vendors must build their products embeds the standard setter's product in an ecosystem. This technology embedding is distinct from what's called *vendor lock-in*, which revolves around a commercial arrangement with restrictive terms. Standard setting is possible in either a superior technology or a dominant market position. There are many examples of great companies that embedded their technology across an ecosystem, from SAP, to Oracle, to Microsoft.

Standards, as communicated through documentation and training, give protocol, data, product, personnel, and process lock-in.

- *Protocol* lock-in comes from other vendors needing to adhere to a specific system architecture, such as data formats or model structure. This **decreases** switching costs for **potential** customers, making it easy for them to adopt a product adhering to the standard. This **increases** switching costs for **current** customers because it may be expensive to search for a provider that works with the protocol or reformat data. Perhaps the best-known example of this in the data world is Microsoft Excel. Microsoft has tremendous lock-in for this analytics product because the format is proprietary. Making protocols transparent and editable—for example, by open sourcing software—is one of the main ways to get others in the industry to adopt a standard.

- *Data* lock-in might come from other vendors needing to send data through a specific system and allowing data collection on the way. This may increase lock-in if that data trains an intelligent system to be better than competitors' systems. For instance, SAP is the hub of supply-chain data, and anyone developing a new piece of software to help understand a supply chain has to work with SAP's data protocols.

- *Product* lock-in comes from other vendors needing to run their software in a specific interface. This increases lock-in because there are fewer differences between competing product interfaces. For example, Salesforce offers a CRM system with lots of features and allows vendors to build apps on top of this CRM, but only if those apps run in the Salesforce interface. This makes it hard for customers to see additional value in apps running inside Salesforce.

- *Personnel* lock-in comes from the customers' staff getting used to using a product based on its architecture, data, or interface. This increases switching costs from competitors. For example, Oracle trained—directly and indirectly—many developers to use its proprietary database querying languages over the last few decades, and those developers can now move with ease between other companies that also use Oracle databases.

- *Process* lock-in comes from requiring implementation partners to adhere to an order of operations to control quality. This increases switching costs because current customers will not switch to an alternative vendor unless they have an agreement with a partner—often known as a systems integrator (SI) or independent software vendor (ISV)—that adheres to that order of operations. For example, VMWare, a cloud computing and virtualization software company, trains systems integrators to properly install their hardware in computing facilities. Customers are unlikely to take a risk on a new systems integrator to build them a whole new facility.

Staging

The question of when and how to pursue standardization to get customer lock-in is perhaps one of the most important when setting a technology company's product and marketing strategies. Computers are complicated enough to need standards across an ecosystem to work together. When to set the standard depends on whether it is a new market or mature.

Companies creating a new market generally promote standardization so that their technology is adopted widely. Standards not only make it easy for customers to integrate their existing systems—for example, by putting data into their AI-First product in a standard data format—but also they open the door for third-party developers to build complementary features such as a simple interface that lets customers tweak parameters in an AI model, thus expanding a product's market from technical to nontechnical customers. Standards make it easier for companies to position themselves as generalists that know something about a novel technology by showing implementations built by others according to those standards. Generalist firms capable of custom implementations thrive at this point because there is fragmentation in the product space. We see start-ups, for instance, hold off on focusing on a vertical at this stage of a market's life cycle.

Dominant companies in mature markets tend to demote standardization, promote fragmentation, or enforce a highly detailed standard to reduce competition from new entrants. Standards ease the way for newcomers to enter mature markets because they can quickly build a product using all the specifications in the standard and get it out to customers who are already accustomed to that standard. Demoting standardization makes it hard for a new entrant to build a product to which customers can switch easily. Promoting fragmentation causes customer confusion to the point of resorting to the dominant vendor with the most stable architecture.

Detailed standards decrease an ability for new entrants to differentiate on product features because features are dictated by the standard, causing customers to choose the dominant vendor based on something other than product features, such as implementation services or a good relationship. At this point, highly specialized firms may have the only product that is mature enough to adhere to every part of the standard. They will thrive.

Considering when to execute on standardization initiatives involves recognizing who has leverage in a given market. This might be those lowest in the chain, such as the manufacturer of hardware on which software runs. Everyone needs the hardware manufacturer to adopt the standard; otherwise none of the software will work. The computing chip manufacturer NVIDIA has such leverage in the machine learning market. The California-based company has, on many measures, the highest performance computer chips on which to run many types of ML models. Developers learn CUDA, a programming language developed by NVIDIA, in order to write instructions for NVIDIA's computer chips. Once developers are using CUDA, the company can show them other new software that it wants to sell. Figuring out who controls a key user interface or data pipeline bottleneck may be key to this consideration; for example, *enterprise resource planning (ERP)* software collects and thus contains data about product inventory. Leverage may also be on the buyer's side instead of the supplier's side, in that governments and other large purchasers can influence standard setting to an extent that the industry standards work well with their existing infrastructure.

Finally, alliances of corporate and noncorporate organizations tend to set standards for whole industries, so forming such alliances is a valuable strategic competency. This was the case in the telecommunications industry with the International Telecommunication Union (ITU), an alliance created by the United Nations to set the standards for mobile device communication through a very long series of meetings with the world's major radio tower, cell-phone, and networking device manufacturers, in addition to the telecommunications service providers. We see this in the software world, too, often with a corporate sponsor, as in the case of Google's sponsoring Kubernetes (a way to write software so that it can be deployed on multiple computers in the cloud at once) and Keras (a set of frameworks on which to build ML models), which allows it to consolidate internal development efforts on those standards, invest in a growing community, attract talent to build better products according to these standards, growing the community, and so on, in a positive reinforcement loop.

Ultimately, customers will refuse to adopt features that lock them into a product unless those features add a lot of value, so pushing adoption of those features too early—when they haven't yet demonstrated an obvious benefit—is futile. On the other hand, there is a risk of losing customers if they're pushed to adopt those features too late, by which time they may be interested in new entrants offering the same features. Adopting restrictive terms of use early, when technology is novel, is a way to protect intellectual property, while loosening terms later, when competitors' technology catches up, is a wise approach for expanding the ecosystem around a product by letting other products integrate. This is both a product strategy and financial calculus: the product calculus is about whether customers have functional alternatives; the financial calculus is about whether it's profitable to expand usage with current customers or by acquiring new customers—who may be hard to bring into the fold on relatively restrictive terms and require deep integration.

Ecosystem

Compatibility

Compatibility—introducing a new product that works with the products customers already use—is an important consideration for AI-First companies needing data from other applications in order to train underlying models. Truly novel, revolutionary, and vertically integrated products can be incompatible with existing products because the value offered is so obvious and so complete that customers are willing to adopt them, despite wholesale changes to computing, data, and staffing. Indeed, revolutionary products may have such novel technology that it's impossible to make it compatible with existing technologies. The Apple iPhone is an example of this: developers were prohibited from designing apps for the iPhone for the first few years, preventing people from using Microsoft Outlook and other popular apps, but the product was so revolutionary that it sold millions of units. However, it is very difficult to create a truly novel product and vertically integrate everything a customer may need into that product from day one. Therefore, some consideration of compatibility is often necessary when setting a market entry strategy. Less novel, evolutionary, and horizontal products must be compatible with existing products because the value they offer is dependent upon a customer's already using an existing product. The key is making an honest assessment of the relative novelty of a product, its degree of vertical integration with respect to other products in the market, and its dependencies. Products may be evolutionary to start, such as a plug-in to a system of record, and become revolutionary after collecting data through that plug-in to build a truly novel, predictive system—a prime example being an analytics dashboard that evolves to a complete decision-making system.

Individual companies don't have to do all the work to make products compatible with others. Incumbents may decide to build integrations because they want the incremental features that new products provide. Technologically, incompatibility can be bridged by intermediate technologies or licensing intellectual property to key collaborators to both enable and incentivize them to build integrations. There are many ways to short-circuit compatibility, and providing *too much* compatibility may allow competitors to steal customers. Picking when to let other developers build on top of a product is a consideration to constantly revisit.

Complementarity

Investing in complementary products, either by building them or having an ecosystem of developers build them, increases the customer value. SAS and Tableau are two companies producing analytics products that augment other analytics products with extra statistical and visualization functions, respectively. Investing engineering resources in developing complementary products calls for a balance between whether they increase competition for the core product and what they're worth to customers. Encourage others to develop complementary products that don't compete against the core product but consider developing those products where the complementary product may evolve into something competitive.

Workflow products without intelligent features are often precursors to AI-First products because they consolidate data into one place—a system of record. For example, a product that predicts what inventory to order needs inventory data from the system of record to train models generating predictions. Where there isn't a precursor product—a system of record holding the data—then building that workflow product and giving it away for free to get the data could more deeply embed the AI-First product.

First-Mover Advantage

Getting to market first is a way to build a competitive advantage, albeit one that's debated in the field of management strategy. However, it is of peculiar application to AI-First startups: the pros are powerful, and the cons don't apply.

First movers collect scarce assets, build technological leadership, and create switching costs before competitors. AI-First companies do the same. First movers collect scarce assets before competitors; AI-First companies collect data (and secure exclusive access to it) before competitors, using one of the many methods outlined in Chapter 3, "Getting the Data." Google collected and stored large amounts of search data before its competitors, and that makes its search product the best today. First movers build technological leadership over competitors by getting a head start on technology research and development; AI-First companies build intelligent systems that are better than competitors' systems both by collecting data and by developing ways to design intelligent systems that yield accurate predictions. Importantly, the research that precedes novel AI development requires data to run experiments. Google started driving cars to collect data and investing in research on autonomous driving before its competitors, and arguably has the most promising autonomous vehicles today. First movers create switching costs by integrating with incumbent systems and benefiting from the uncertainty that surrounds new entrants; AI-First companies create switching costs by centralizing customers' data into their own databases and proving superior model accuracy. Google centralizes and secures data across consumers' email, location, and documents to generate the best recommendations for things to buy, places to go, and even phrases to write. AI-First companies are first movers.

Moving first sometimes hurts a company's competitive position because potential competitors benefit from the technology the first mover develops. Increased certainty around underlying standards also gives customers more knowledge about how to use the new technology. Debatably, AI-First companies aren't subject to this potential downside of moving first. Free riders can't benefit from technology developed by first movers because they don't have the data owned by the AI-First company. For example, there are many promising AI-based methods to improve search, but the path to developing a search superior to Google's seems intractable because it's hard to identify the meaning of phrases—especially those that aren't used much—without a lot of search data to train models. Free-riding copycats need both the technology and the data. Customer certainty around underlying standards is less relevant to AI-First companies than it is to standard technology companies because the benefit of the technology accrues through the accuracy of the prediction rather than through interoperability with existing systems. Customers don't buy a system that predicts which sales lead to chase next because it integrates with the most CRMs, they just need it to integrate with the CRM they currently use and get good leads. AI-First companies enjoy the benefit of more customer certainty as the accuracy of their system improves with the addition of real-world data. Finally, first movers sometimes see their initial lead erode as second movers adapt more quickly to a shift in market needs. Again, this disadvantage of being a first mover doesn't apply to AI-First companies because intelligent systems constantly adapt to incoming data. Intelligent systems are inherently dynamic, adapting to competitors as they reach market.

Branding

Consumers buy into brands that they trust and like. Brands build trust through consistency and are liked for their usability. They do this through personalization.

Customers value consistent product experiences because they get the same payoff every time they spend money. McDonald's is a famous example of a brand built on consistency: you get the same burger in Boston as you do in Berlin. This is also true for business brands. For example, IBM's customers value the professionalism of consulting services that come with purchasing the company's software. AI-First companies are in a uniquely good position to provide consistent product experiences because the products run off algorithms. There are ways in which those algorithms—being probabilistic—can deliver inconsistent results, but such outcomes can be avoided with overriding rules-based systems. Explainability and audit features can also increase the *perception* of consistency by customers.

Usable products are simply those that are easy to manipulate: well-designed handles that fit your hand, buttons where you expect them to be, and no need for instructions. AI-First companies are in a uniquely good position to make usable products because the product is often a recommendation, and that recommendation is generated from contextual data, so the product is context appropriate. Delivering a recommendation or decision just at the time it's needed makes it usable, and that's what AI-First products do right.

Consistency and usability seem to be in opposition to each other because consistency means delivering the same product every time, no matter the context, whereas usability depends on the context. You generally don't want ice cream in freezing weather even if it objectively tastes exactly the same as it does when it's hot outside. The way to achieve both consistency and usability is through personalization. Getting data on how customers use the product to personalize the delivery of that product is challenging because of the many data points: every click, movement of the mouse, and purchase can be recorded. AI-First companies have an advantage because intelligent systems can process lots of data points. This nuanced power affords AI-First companies brand-building powers—intelligent systems can analyze large amounts of product-usage data to personalize products at scale—which in turn better enables those companies to get more customers and capture more data.

LEVERAGING THE LOOP AGAINST INCUMBENTS

Aggregating advantages puts AI-First companies in a position to subordinate incumbents. This section provides perspectives on positioning AI-First products against incumbents in order to win over their customers.

From Databases to Intelligent Applications

New technology borrows from old, first integrating it and then eventually subordinating it. *Intelligent applications*, meaning applications delivering the output of an AI, need data, and that data lives in *legacy applications,* meaning the applications that customers use today. Here's how to borrow from and then subordinate legacy applications.

Many years ago, only technical people could use a database. The software era of the 1990s allowed nontechnical people to work with databases through Microsoft Access. After that came cloud-based applications that had everyone adding data from everywhere as part of their daily workflow—without even thinking they were manipulating databases. Today those cloud applications are effectively the databases behind software because the databases themselves are so many levels below the application that no one directly interacts with the database.

However, these legacy applications were built in an era where storing data was expensive, so they tended to store only what was necessary. Three things changed:

1. data is cheaper to store;

2. workers execute their entire workflow online, generating more data about what they're doing and how they're making decisions; and

3. the methods for learning over that data improved.

AI becomes possible when data is cheaper to store, there's more of it, and there are methods to make sense of it. This poses a tremendous opportunity in the AI-First Century: capture the data "exhaust" (anything recorded when customers perform operations in an application, such as clicking buttons and changing values) from existing systems of record (the "single source of truth" for a business function), and build AI on top.

Better Data Collection, Better Products

Salesforce is a system of record, and the apps on top are intelligent applications. Let's think a little more about the differences between these applications with respect to how data is input and what that allows.

	SYSTEM OF RECORD	INTELLIGENT APPLICATION
Data entry	Explicit	Implicit
Input user	Humans	Machines
Input timing	Post facto	Live
Data type	Structured	Unstructured
Data categorization	Fields	Exhaust

Let's expand the right column above to see how intelligent applications allow for new ways to work with data.

	TYPE	BENEFIT
Data entry	Implicit	Increase in contextual data gathered from public and ancillary sources, made available for later analysis.
Input user	Machines	Reduced time required to input data, so that you can do real work. No more updating Salesforce every month.
Input timing	Live	Ability to act on data in real time. Data is uploaded from the system of record, predictive models are applied, and actionable insights made available to the user.
Data type	Unstructured	Deep learning over unstructured data to turn it into structured data and extract predictive features. There's just not enough data about most jobs available for the training of deep learning models.
Data categorization	Exhaust	Higher accuracy by removing reporting bias. A machine-generated summary of the last email from a sales lead is perhaps more indicative of a likelihood to close a deal with that lead than a salesperson's subjective opinion expressed in a single, categorical input.

Intelligent applications get more fresh, varied, and voluminous data than data put into systems of record.

Opportunities

Many domains are devoid of truly intelligent workflow applications. That is, intelligent applications that run ML algorithms over a combination of rich input data, exhaust data, and external data to make predictions, or, ideally, decisions for the customers. The opportunity for AI-First companies is to build applications like this, as illustrated by the following examples:

- CRM that predictively manages leads for sales, marketing, and fundraising in narrow domains;

- inventory management software that shows when inventory is likely to be out and orders more, ahead of time;

- supply-chain tracking that predicts breaks in the supply chain and suggests work-arounds; and

- product management tools that automatically collect feature ideas (and bugs to fix) from customer support tickets.

Now is the time to consider how to build an intelligent application on top of a system of record.

The Talent Loop

Building intelligent systems requires intelligent people. Hiring the best ML engineers, researchers, and data scientists is a prerequisite to building the most intelligent systems. The best people in this field want to work with the best data because it's hard for them to do much without good data. The best data usually means the most data.

More data makes ML work more productive, attracting better ML people, generating more useful models, and thus more data, making ML work more productive, and so on, in a self-reinforcing loop.

Promoting the value of data assets to potential candidates can kick off this *talent loop*. Some candidates want to see lots of data, some want to see a dataset most relevant to their research, and others want a dataset with which they can change the world. For example, collecting a proprietary dataset that may help solve an important problem, such as cancer, could attract high-quality talent. Identifying and articulating data and engineering problems to candidates can be a hiring advantage. Figuring out how to attract the best people can depend on the data you have.

THE TALENT LOOP

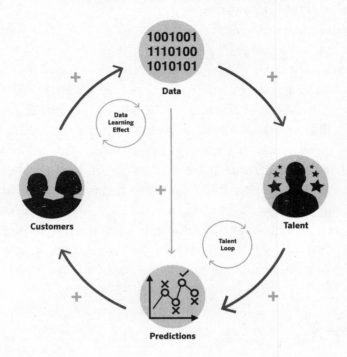

CONCLUSION:
SEQUENCING FOR COMPETING

I think that the biggest commercial opportunity in this AI-First Century is to create companies that completely automate valuable services to society. However, you don't start by automating the provision of those services, you start by manually providing those services. You don't start by building technology; you start by building understanding. Acquiring a services company is often a better way to start an AI-First company than fundraising for a technology company. Starting with a low-margin, manual business in order to acquire data is an odd proposition for someone looking to raise venture capital to build a high-margin software business. But it might make sense to someone who ultimately wants to capture all the value created by automation.

Vertical integration allows for virtual control over adoption and capturing value through ROI-based pricing, but it can be very costly to implement. There are other, lucrative ways to price AI-First products based on how data moves around them, as well as ways to position these products in the part of the value chain containing the biggest profit opportunity. Getting customer lock-in by setting industry standards, supporting an ecosystem, or building a brand can emulate some of the benefits of vertical integration, but the reality is that sometimes just being first is all it takes to win, especially if it kicks off a self-reinforcing loop. Aggregating advantages puts companies in a position to become the intelligent application that subordinates incumbents. AI-First companies are aggregating, subordinating, and disrupting incumbents every day.

PLAYBOOK

- **Vertical integration gets more data, revenue, and profit.** Providing the whole package for a customer positions AI-First companies to obtain feedback data, price their products based on ROI, and improve margins.

- **Pricing changes with AI.** AI-First companies can charge customers based on data contribution, rate of using the product, frequency of model updates, developing predictive features, and, ultimately, ROI. Underwriting to ROI is the ideal business model for AI-First companies.

- **AI-First disruption comes in three phases.** Take customers from incumbents with (1) lower prices, (2) a higher degree of personalization, and (3) more automation.

- **Aggregating data creates new products.** AI-First companies can aggregate data to devise new products, whether they are making sense of large volumes of data or inventing something totally new. AI-First companies aggregate and integrate forward, getting data from a database and building an intelligent system that customers use every day.

- **Data generates lock-in.** Data formats can lock customers into products.

- **Consider compatibility.** Data moves between products in an ecosystem so compatibility with other products can help new entrants get data into their own product that can then be used to train an AI.

- **Support complements.** Third parties can create complementary products that contribute data to an ecosystem, ultimately delivering more value to customers.

- **First-mover advantage works well for AI-First companies.** The pros are powerful, and the cons don't apply. Accumulating data before competitors do kicks off the DLE, building an unassailable head start.

- **AI-First companies have unique brand-building powers.** Intelligent systems can analyze large amounts of product-usage data to personalize products at scale. This brand-building power positions AI-First companies to sign more customers and capture more data.

- **Subordinate incumbents.** Intelligent applications borrow from and then subordinate legacy applications, collecting data and recruiting talent to work with that data in an entirely different way than incumbent companies do.

CONCLUSION

Building an AI-First company requires putting AI first on every agenda. This book puts AI first in discussions about strategy (positioning, pricing, competing) and tactics (on modeling, monitoring, and metrics). Executing on this puts data learning effects in motion.

Your learning about AI-First companies can also benefit from data learning effects.

> data learning effects = economies of scale to data + data processing capabilities + data network effects.

Imagine, if you will, that your fresh data is the new vocabulary and frameworks presented in this book. The processing happens as you think about them at work. Each paragraph, illustration, and example adds to the network of information. This book got the flywheel started. There's more to keep it going and to keep the loop *growing.* You can find more input in the form of supplementary materials, worksheets, and courses. You can keep processing these inputs in your day job. And you can add a lot more nodes to the network by joining online communities.

AI-First companies put AI first. You've put AI first in your learning, so now you can put AI first in your company's strategy, budget, and staff meetings. You can go into your next project with a Lean-AI mindset, even when starting small. You can lead implementations for customers with practices that ensure acceptance of AI, install automatic management systems, and set up metrics to monitor progress. Learning and accumulating information across your company will allow you to consistently achieve good results and improve upon your decisions. Eventually your company will build machines that help at a greater scale and speed. You can outpace your competitors through vertical integration, disruption, positioning through standardization, aggregation, and subordination.

Remember, it's not too late; we're just over halfway through the AI-First Century. You can still build third-wave tools to give us all leverage. We got here by doing that with and for one another, and we're all in this together.

ACKNOWLEDGMENTS

I WOULD LIKE TO ACKNOWLEDGE the contributions of certain people who formed this book, knowingly or not.

The founders and CEOs for whom I work teach me about intelligent systems more than any other group of people I know or articles I read. These pioneers are breaking new ground and I'm fortunate to be privy to what they find. They are Jude Allred, Jason Arbon, Jodok Batlogg, Michael Brand, Francois Chaubard, Adrien Cohen, Alex Dalyac, John DeNero, Dave Elkington, Nick Elprin, Eli Finkelshteyn, Anthony Goldbloom, Gregg Golembeski, Spence Green, Ben Hamner, Matthew Hudson, Josh James, Benji Koltai, Justin Liu, Christian Lutz, Alex MacCaw, Simon MacGibbon, Dan McCormick, Adriano Quiroga, Razvan Ranca, Bryan Smith, Joel Spolsky, Christian Steinruecken, Cozmin Ududec, Bob van Llujt, and David Wilkinson. Thank you for letting me sit in the passenger seat as you drive to the frontier of knowledge.

The team at Zetta (past and present)—James Alcorn, Jocelyn Goldfein, Mark Gorenberg, Kanu Gulati, Ivy Nguyen, and Dylan

ACKNOWLEDGMENTS

Reid—teach me about turning technology into companies of consequence. Some of the ideas in this book stemmed from our daily discussions, growing over the nights and weekends into this book.

Noah Schwartzberg at Portfolio is an excellent editor and a kind man. He gave this book a compelling purpose and an attractive form, pushing the pedagogical purpose forward. Thank you for your patience, enthusiasm, and generosity.

Niki Papadopoulos saw the pedagogical purpose of this book within minutes of us meeting and supported it through to the point of making sure it got the support it needs, across the whole Portfolio team.

Nina Rodriguez-Marty challenged and supported me in making the book more understandable. This was a big job that involved defining hundreds of technical terms and reading thousands of pages. Thank you for your diligence, determination, and deliberate feedback.

Philip Bashe's careful consideration of every word in this book also led to it being more understandable and his skillful editing made the knowledge herein far more accessible.

Jim Levine also immediately saw the purpose, platform, and my passion behind this book. His professionalism and perspective in all matters was most valuable. I would not have wanted to publish this book without his counsel.

Charles Ferguson encouraged me to publish this book, advised me as to how, and—crucially—connected ideas across technology strategy and intelligent systems to help me conceive of data learning effects. Thank you for dealing with my deliberations from Inverness to Verona, and the many towns in between.

Seth Benzell's input led to many of the equations that articulate data learning effects herein and provided technical corrections to the various articulations of network effects. Thank you to Dean Eckles for introducing us.

Lauren Humphrey assisted me with earlier versions of the book and her research on competitive strategy helped me figure out what's worth writing.

Fabiola Reina and Alejandra Miranda took my ideas and turned them into artwork that makes the concepts in this book far easier to understand than my words could do alone.

The reviewers: James Allworth, James Boyers, Keiran Brown, Narayan Chowdhury, Anthony Goldbloom, Mark Gorenberg, Matthew Hudson, Nikolas Kirby, Ben Mathes, Tim Olshansky, Michael Overell, Emma Perera, David Perrell, Giorgia Rossi, Jason Smale, Richard Stebbing, Christian Steinruecken, Mark Tanner, Tom Tunguz, and Michael Walsh. Each of you spent a lot of time reading early versions of this book, which were not easy to read. James Allworth catalyzed a complete change in the structure of the book, giving me the feedback that guided the first major re-write of the book. Keiran Brown opened up my eyes to some important literature on competitive strategy. Narayan Chowdhury shares my passion for the history of the field and wrote an informative piece that I read while denoting the AI-First Century. Anthony Goldbloom provided examples that informed the "Lean AI" chapter and others. Mark Gorenberg helped with the setup of key terms and keeping the focus on start-ups. Nikolas Kirby catalyzed a major, structural change that made this book more practical and re-minded me of what we learned as debaters: signpost. Ben Mathes helped me conceive of the model management loop and provided technical corrections to key terms. Michael Overell provided the perspective of an entrepreneur in a thoughtful, structured, and actionable way. David Perrell injected the introduction and wording of later chapters with life. Emma Perera gave the sort of sensible and weighty advice only a publisher and best friend can. Tom Tunguz encouraged me to publish this book the right way and introduced me to the first publisher I met, in addition to providing feedback on earlier chapters. Giorgia Rossi was there from the beginning to the end: encouraging me to put pen to paper, holding my hand as I took the first steps, and providing an entrepreneur's view of the completed manuscript. Jason Smale offered lessons applicable to the "Lean AI," "AI-First Teams," and "Managing the Models" chapters from his experience managing technology teams. Richard Stebbing and Christian Steinruecken provided crucial, technical corrections and feedback throughout.

The people of Point Reyes (California) and Bassano del Grappa (Veneto) welcomed me into their towns, homes, taverns, and farms. You also welcomed my bicycle on your trails and roads. Your hospitality provided much-needed support, energy, and solace throughout this project.

Mum, for providing advice on everything from where to place an adverb (nowhere) and of the legal variety. Your sensibility and positivity in all matters ground what I do, every day—as they have for my whole life.

Dad, for keeping me on the road—wheels rolling and head high—whatever turn I take.

Brother, for teaching me about the natural world, evolution, and our values.

GLOSSARY

A/B TEST: testing for user preferences by randomly showing two different variants of a product (i.e., variants A and B) to different groups of users; also known as a split test

ACYCLIC: jumping between points rather than going through points in the same pattern each time

AGENT-BASED MODEL: model that generates the actions of agents and interactions with other agents given the agent's properties, incentives, and environmental constraints

AGGREGATION THEORY: the theory that new entrants in a market can aggregate existing quantities in that market; for example, data points, to create new and valuable products

APPLICATION PROGRAMMING INTERFACE: a set of functions that allows applications to communicate with other applications, either to use a feature or fetch data; effectively, a structured way for software to communicate with other pieces of software

AREA UNDERNEATH THE CURVE (AUC): the integral of the ROC curve

BLOCKCHAIN: decentralized and distributed public ledger of transactions

CLUSTERING TOOL: using unsupervised machine learning to group similar objects

COMPLEMENTARY DATA: new data that increases the value of existing data

CONCAVE PAYOFF: decreasing dividends from using a product

CONCEPT DRIFT: when the idea behind the subject of a prediction changes based on observations

CONSUMER APP: software application primarily used by individuals (rather than businesses)

CONTRIBUTION MARGIN: average price per unit minus labor and quality control costs associated with that unit

CONVEX PAYOFF: increasing dividends from using a product

COST LEADERSHIP: a form of competitive advantage that comes from having the lowest cost of production with respect to competitors in a given industry

CRYPTOGRAPHY: writing and solving codes

CRYPTO TOKEN: representation of an asset that is kept on a blockchain

CUSTOMER RELATIONSHIP MANAGEMENT SOFTWARE: software that stores and manipulates data about customers

CUSTOMER SUPPORT AGENT: employee that is paid to respond to customer support tickets

CUSTOMER SUPPORT TICKET: message from user of a product requesting help in using that product

CYBERNETICS: the science of control and communication in machines and living things

DATA: facts and statistics collected together for reference or analysis

DATA ANALYST: person who sets up dashboards, visualizes data, and interprets model outputs

DATA DRIFT: (1) when the distribution on which a prediction is based changes such that it no longer represents observed reality; or (2) when the data on which a prediction is based changes such that some of it is no longer available or properly formed

DATA ENGINEER: person who cleans data, creates automated data management tools, maintains the data catalogue, consolidates data assets, incorporates new data sources, maintains data pipelines, sets up links to external data sources, and more

DATA EXHAUST: data collected when users perform operations in an application, for example clicking buttons and changing values

DATA INFRASTRUCTURE ENGINEER: person who chooses the right database, sets up databases, moves data between them, and manages infrastructure cost and more

DATA LABELING: adding a piece of information to a piece of data

DATA LEARNING EFFECT: the automatic compounding of information

DATA LEARNING LOOP: the endogenous and continuous generation of proprietary data from an intelligent system that provides the basis of the next generation of that intelligent system

DATA NETWORK: set of data that is built by a group of otherwise unrelated entities, rather than a single entity

DATA NETWORK EFFECT: the increase in marginal benefit that comes from adding a new data point to an existing collection of data; the marginal benefit is defined in terms of informational value

DATA PRODUCT MANAGER: person who incorporates the data needs of the model with the usability intentions of the product designers and preferences of users in order to prioritize product features that collect proprietary data

DATA SCIENTIST: person who sets up and runs data science experiments

DATA STEWARD: person responsible for ensuring compliance to data storage standards

DEEP LEARNING: artificial neural network with multiple layers

DEFENSIBILITY: the relative ability to protect a source of income; for example, an income-generating asset

DIFFERENTIAL PRIVACY: system for sharing datasets without revealing the individual data points

DIMENSIONALITY REDUCTION: transforming data (using a method such as principal component analysis) to reduce the measures associated with each data point

DISRUPTION THEORY: the theory that new entrants in a market can appropriate customers from incumbent suppliers by selling a specialized product to a niche segment of customers at a fraction of the cost of the incumbent's product

DRIFT: when a model's concept or data diverges from reality

EDGE: connections between nodes; also called a link or a line

ENTERPRISE RESOURCE PLANNING PRODUCT: software that collects and thus contains data about product inventory

ENTRY-LEVEL DATA NETWORK EFFECT: the compounding marginal benefit that comes from adding new data to an existing collection of data; the marginal benefit is defined in terms of informational value to the model computed over that data

EPOCH: completed pass of the entire training dataset by the machine learning model

ETL (EXTRACT, TRANSFORM, AND LOAD): the three, main steps in moving data from one place to another

EXAMPLE: a single input and output pair from which a machine learning model learns

FEATURE: set of mathematical functions that are fed data to output a prediction

FEDERATED LEARNING: method for training machine learning models across different computers without exchanging data between those computers

FIRST-MOVER: company that collects scarce assets, builds technological leadership, and creates switching costs in a market by virtue of entering that market before other companies

GAUSSIAN MIXTURE MODEL: probabilistic model representing a subset within a set, assuming a normal distribution, without requiring the observed data match the subset

GLOBAL, MULTIUSER MODEL: model that makes predictions about something common to all customers of a given company; this is generally trained on data aggregated across all customers

GRADIENT BOOSTED TREE: method for producing a decision tree in multiple stages according to a loss function

GRAPH: mathematical structure made up of nodes and edges that is typically used to model interactions between objects

HEURISTICS: knowledge acquired by doing

HISTOGRAM: diagram consisting of rectangles whose area is proportional to the frequency of a variable and whose width is equal to the class interval

HORIZONTAL INTEGRATION: the combination in one product of multiple industry-specific functions normally operated by separate products

HUMAN-IN-THE-LOOP SYSTEM: machine learning system that requires human input to generate an output

HYPERPARAMETER: parameter that is used to control the machine learning model

HYPERTEXT MARKUP LANGUAGE: programming language specifically for writing documents to be displayed in a web browser

INCUMBENT: existing market leader

INDEPENDENT SOFTWARE VENDOR: a company that publishes software

INFORMATION: data that resolves uncertainty for the receiver

INSOURCING: finding the resources to complete a task within an existing organization such that it's not necessary to contract new resources to complete that task

INTEGRATOR: software company that builds tools to connect data sources, normalizes data across sources, and updates connections as these sources change

INTELLIGENT APPLICATION: application that runs machine learning algorithms over data to make predictions or decisions

INTERACTIVE MACHINE LEARNING: machine learning models that collect data from a user, put that data into a model, present the model output back to the user, and so on

K-MEANS: unsupervised machine learning method to group objects in a number of clusters based on the cluster with the center point, or average, that's closest to the object

LABEL: the output of a machine learning system based on learning from examples

LAYER: aggregation of neurons; layers can be connected to other layers

LEAN AI: the process of building a small but complete and accurate AI to solve a specific problem

LEARNING EFFECT: the process through which knowledge accumulation leads to an economic benefit

LEGACY APPLICATION: application already in use

LOSS: the quantum of how right or wrong a model was in making a given prediction

LOSS FUNCTION: mathematical function that determines the degree to which the output of a model is incorrect

MACHINE LEARNING: computable algorithms that automatically improve with the addition of novel data

MACHINE LEARNING ENGINEER: person who implements, trains, monitors, and fixes machine learning models

MACHINE LEARNING MANAGEMENT LOOP: automated system for continuous incorporation of real-world data into machine learning models

MACHINE LEARNING RESEARCHER: person who sets up and runs machine learning experiments

MARKETING SEGMENTATION: dividing customers into groups based on similarity

MINIMUM VIABLE PRODUCT: the minimum set of product features that a customer needs for a product to be useful

MOAT: accumulation of assets that form a barrier to other parties that may reduce the income-generating potential of those assets

MONITORING: observing a product to ensure both quality and reliability

NETWORK EFFECT: the increase in marginal benefit that comes from adding a new node to an existing collection of nodes; the marginal benefit is defined in terms of utility to the user of the collection

NEURAL NETWORK: collection of nodes that are connected to each other such that they can transmit signals to each other across the edges of the network, with the strength of the signal depending on the weights on each node and edge

NEXT-LEVEL DATA NETWORK EFFECT: the compounding marginal benefit that comes from adding new data to an existing collection of data; the marginal benefit is defined in terms of the rate of automatic data creation by the model computed over that data

NODE: discrete part of a network that can receive, process, and send signals; also called a vertex or a point

OPTICAL CHARACTER RECOGNITION SOFTWARE: software that turns images into machine-readable text

PARETO OPTIMAL SOLUTION: achieving 80 percent of the optimal solution for 20 percent of the work

PARTIAL PLOT: graph that shows the effect of adding an incremental variable to a function

PERSONALLY IDENTIFIABLE INFORMATION: information that can be linked to a real person

PERTURBATION: deliberately modifying an object, e.g., data

POWER GENERATOR: user that contributes an inordinate amount of data with respect to other users

POWER USER: user that uses a product an inordinate amount with respect to other users

PRECISION: the number of relevant data points retrieved by the model over the total number of data points

PREDICTION USABILITY THRESHOLD: the point at which a prediction becomes useful to a customer

PRICING: product usage; for example, hours spent using a product

PROOF OF CONCEPT: a project jointly conducted by potential customers and vendors of a software product to prove the value theoretically provided by that, in practice

PROPRIETARY INFORMATION: information that is owned by a specific entity and not in the public domain

QUERY LANGUAGE: programming language used to retrieve data from a database

RANDOM FOREST: method for analyzing data that constructs multiple decision trees and outputs the class of objects that occurs most often among all the objects or the average prediction across all of the decision trees

RECALL: the number of relevant data points retrieved by the model over the total number of relevant data points

RECEIVER OPERATING CHARACTERISTIC (ROC) CURVE: plot that shows how well the model performed at different discrimination thresholds, e.g., true and false positive rates

RECURSION: repeated application of a method

REINFORCEMENT LEARNING: ML that learns from objectives

RETURN ON INVESTMENT (ROI): calculated by dividing the return from using an asset by the investment in that asset

ROI-BASED PRICING: pricing that is directly correlated with a rate of return on an investment

SCALE EFFECT: the increase in marginal benefit or reduction in marginal cost that comes from having a higher quantity of the asset or capability that generates the benefit

SCATTER PLOT: graph in which the values of two variables are plotted along two axes, the pattern of the resulting points revealing any correlation present

SCHEME: the form common to all values in a particular table in a database

SECURE MULTIPARTY COMPUTATION: method for jointly computing inputs while keeping the inputs private from the participating computers

SENSOR NETWORK: a collection of devices that collect data from the real world

SIMULATION: method that generates inputs to put through a program to see if that program fails to execute or generates inaccurate outputs

SOFTWARE-AS-A-SERVICE (SAAS): method of delivering software online and licensing that software on a subscription basis

SOFTWARE DEVELOPMENT KIT: tool made by software developers to allow other software developers to build on top of or alongside their software

STATISTICAL PROCESS CONTROL: quality control process that is based on statistical methods

SUPERVISED MACHINE LEARNING: ML that learns from inputs given outputs

SUPPORT VECTOR MACHINE: supervised learning model that classifies new data points by category

SYSTEM OF ENGAGEMENT: system that actively (e.g., through user input) aggregates information about a particular business function

SYSTEM OF RECORD: system that passively aggregates information about a particular business function

SYSTEMS INTEGRATOR: an entity that installs new software systems such that they function with customers' existing systems

TALENT LOOP: the compounding competitive advantage in attracting high-quality personnel that comes from having more high quality data than competitors

TRANSACTIONAL PRICING: pricing that is directly correlated with the quantum of units transacted through a product, for example, number of processed data points or computation cycles

UNSUPERVISED MACHINE LEARNING: ML that learns from inputs without outputs

USAGE-BASED PRICING: pricing that is directly correlated with the quantum of product usage; for example, hours of time spent using a product

USER INTERFACE: set of objects that exist in software that are manipulated to initiate a function in that software

VALUE CHAIN: the process by which a company adds value to an asset; for example, adding value to a data point by processing that data into information, and that information into a prediction

VARIABLE IMPORTANCE PLOT: list of the most important variables in a function in terms of their contribution to a given prediction, or predictive power

VERSIONING: keeping a copy of every form of a model, program, or dataset

VERTICAL INTEGRATION: the combination in one company of multiple stages of production (or points on a value chain) normally operated by separate firms

VERTICAL PRODUCT: software product that is only relevant to users in a particular industry

WATERFALL CHART: data visualization that shows the result of adding or subtracting sequential values in adjacent columns

WEB CRAWLER: program that systematically queries webpages or other documents on the internet; strips out the unnecessary content on those pages, such as formatting; grabs salient data, puts it in a standard document format (e.g., JSON), and puts it in a private data repository

WEIGHT: the relative measure of strength ascribed to nodes and edges in a network; this can be automatically or manually adjusted after learning of a more optimal weight

WORKFLOW APPLICATION: software that takes a sequence of things that someone does in the real world and puts those steps into an interface that allows for data input at each step

ZETTABYTE: 10^21 bytes or 1 trillion gigabytes

INDEX